Growing Up in the Japanese Alps

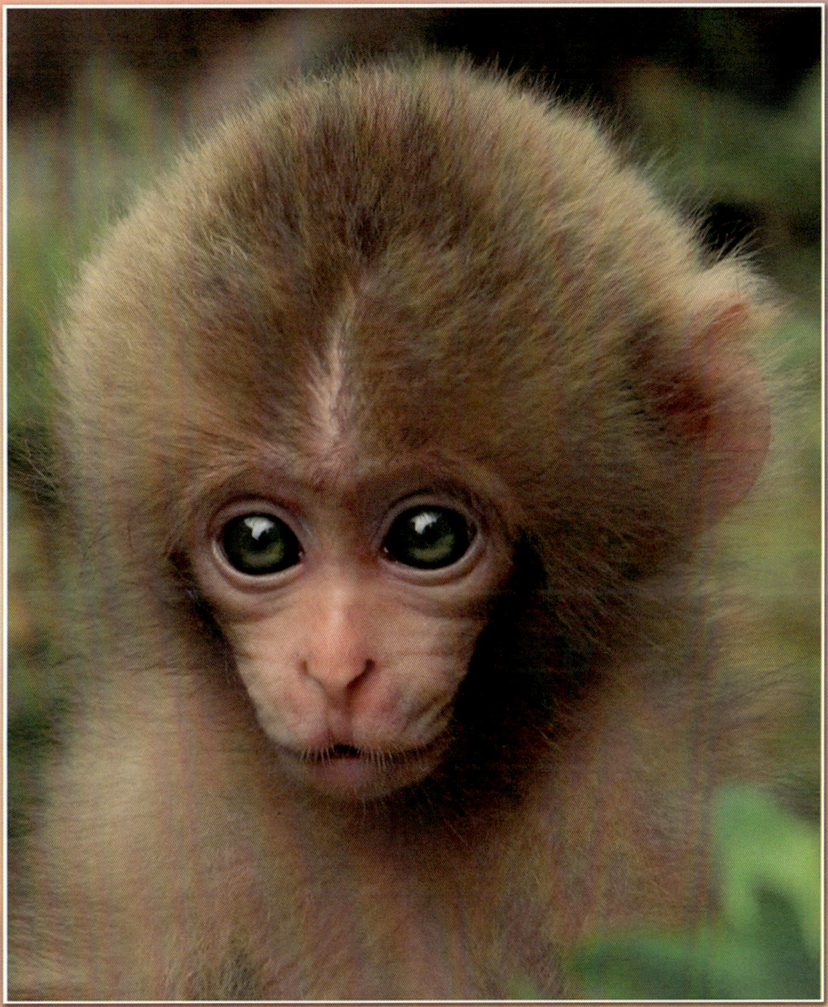

Photography, Artwork, Cover, and Text

by Tim Ostermeyer

www.ostermeyer-photography.com

Welcome to the forest of the Japanese Alps, where I was born.

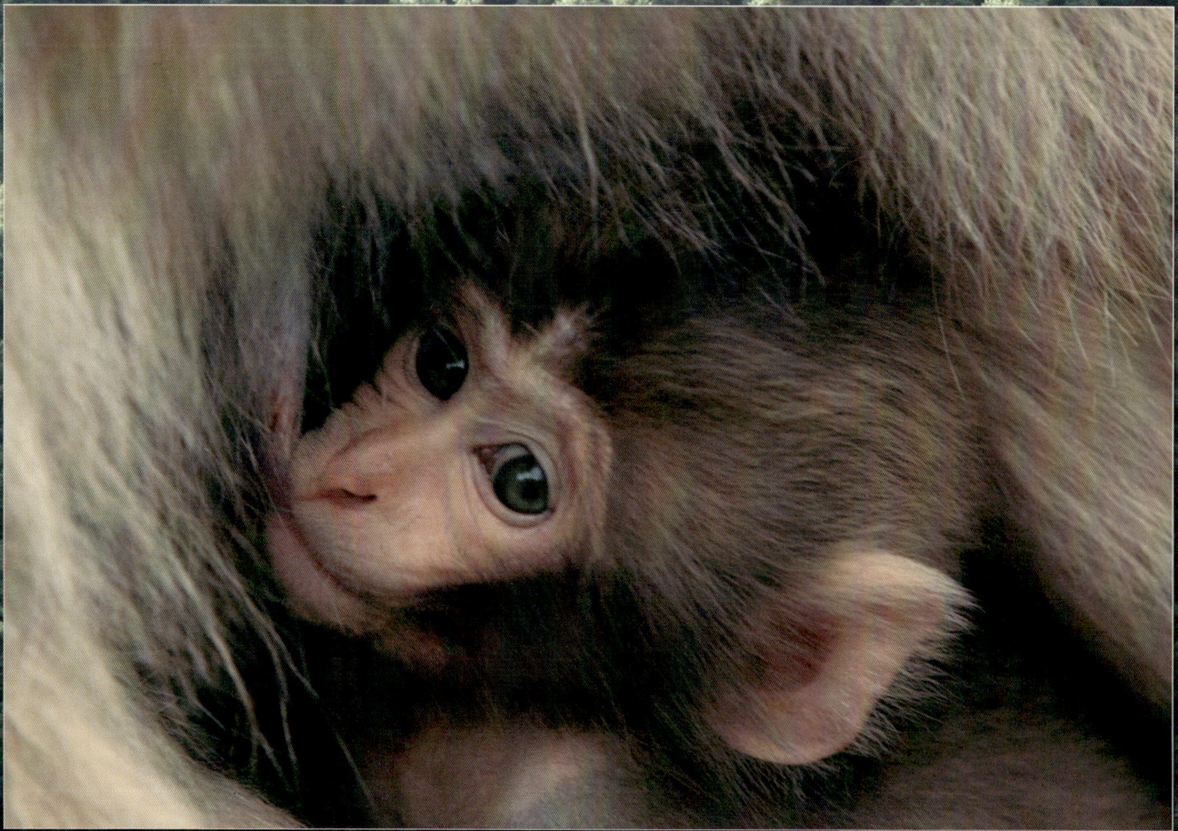

I am only 1 month old. My mother named me "Neptune", because she thinks that I am "out of this world" (very special).

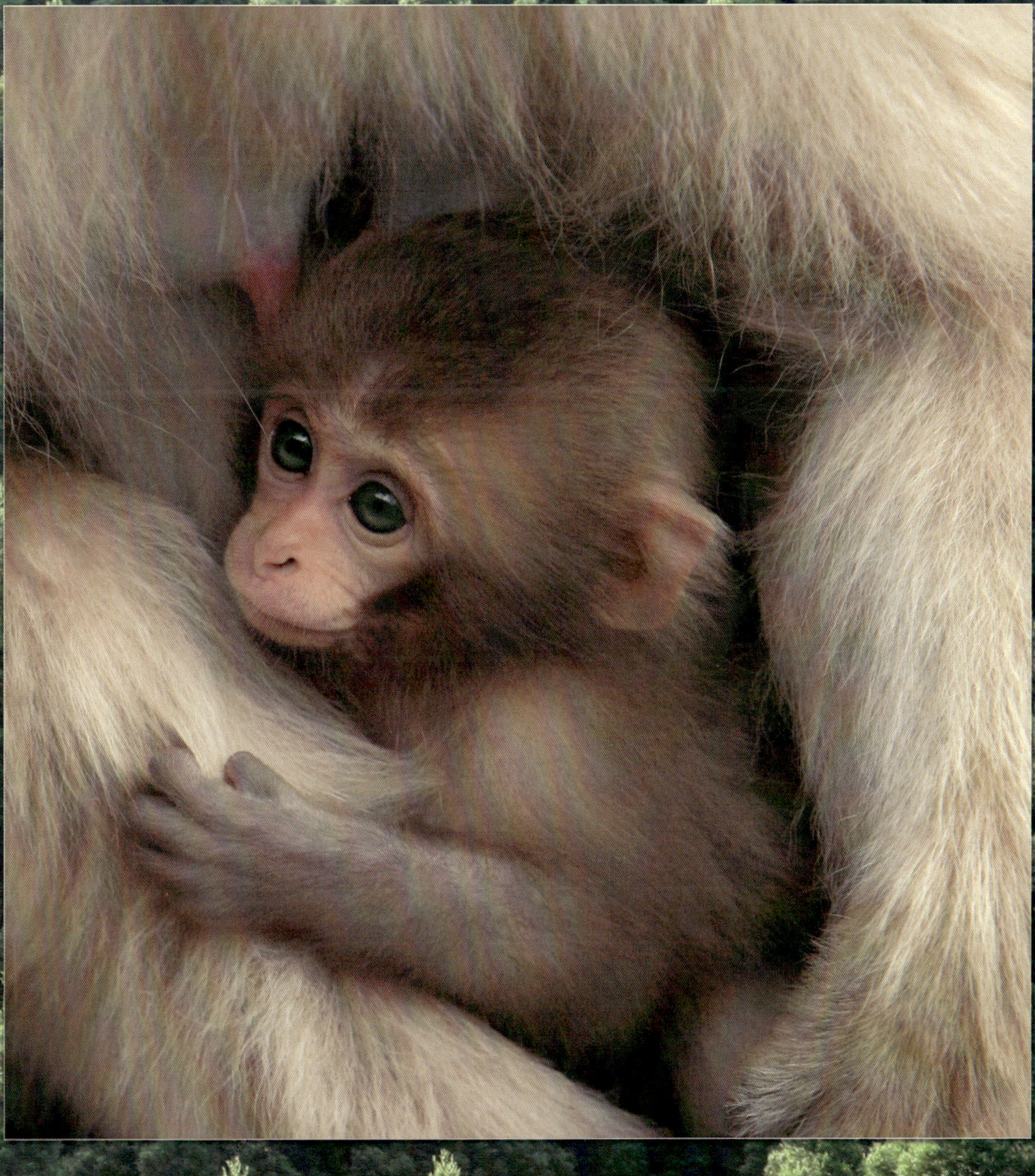

I am a Japanese Snow Monkey.
Do you think that I am cute?

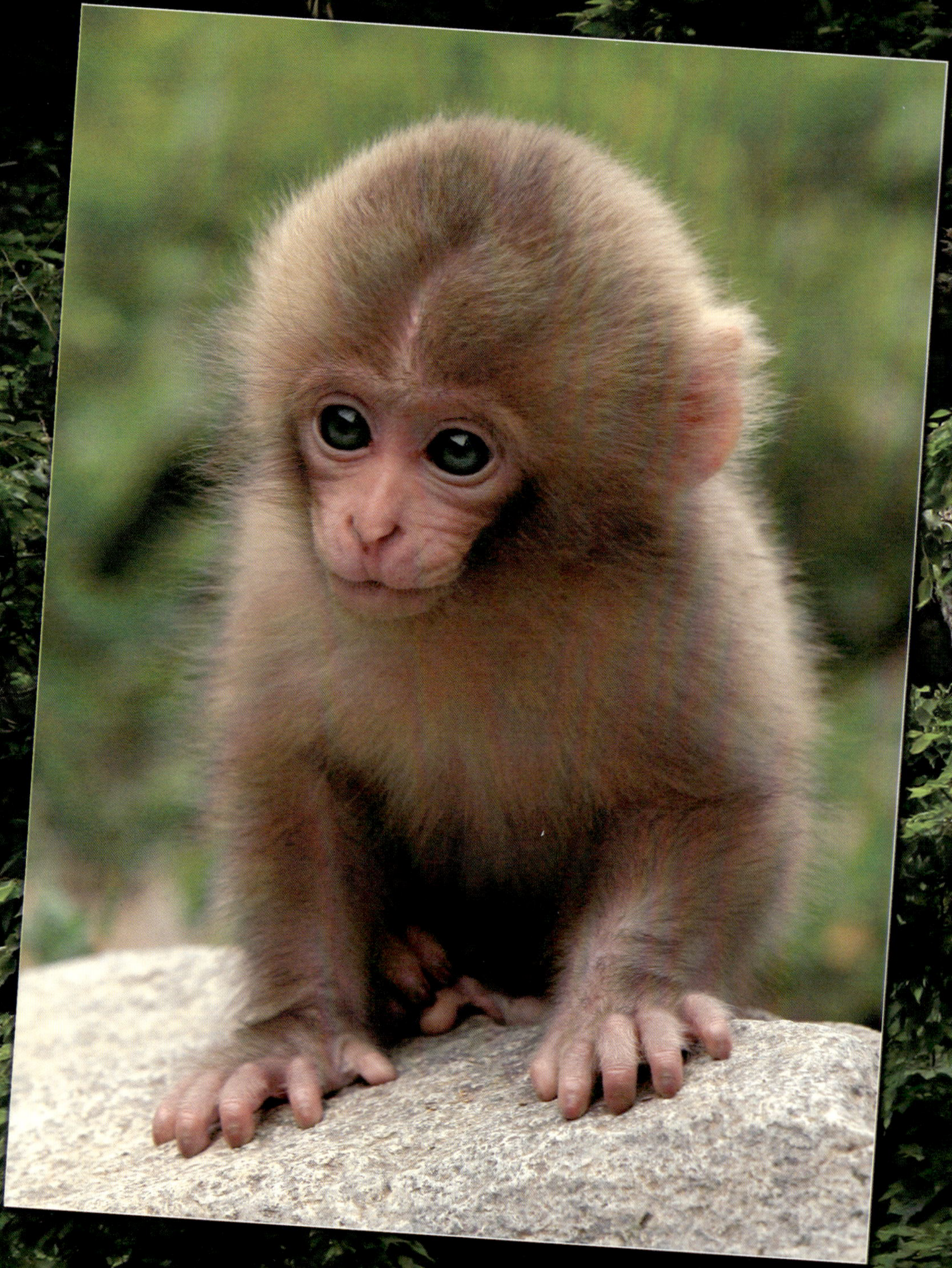

Do you like my little fingers?

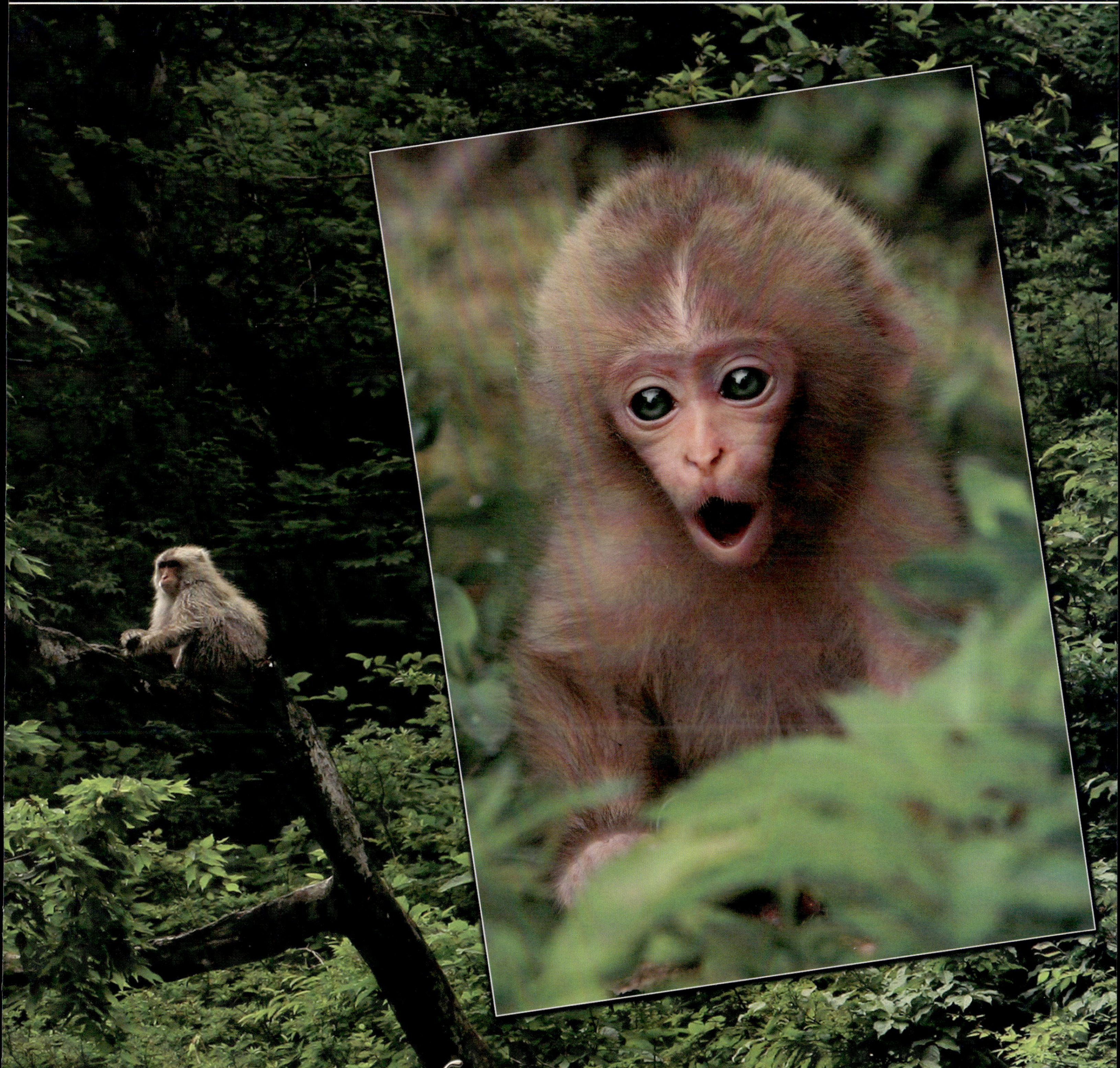

Some monkeys rest on trees.
They enjoy the view,
while staying safe from enemies.

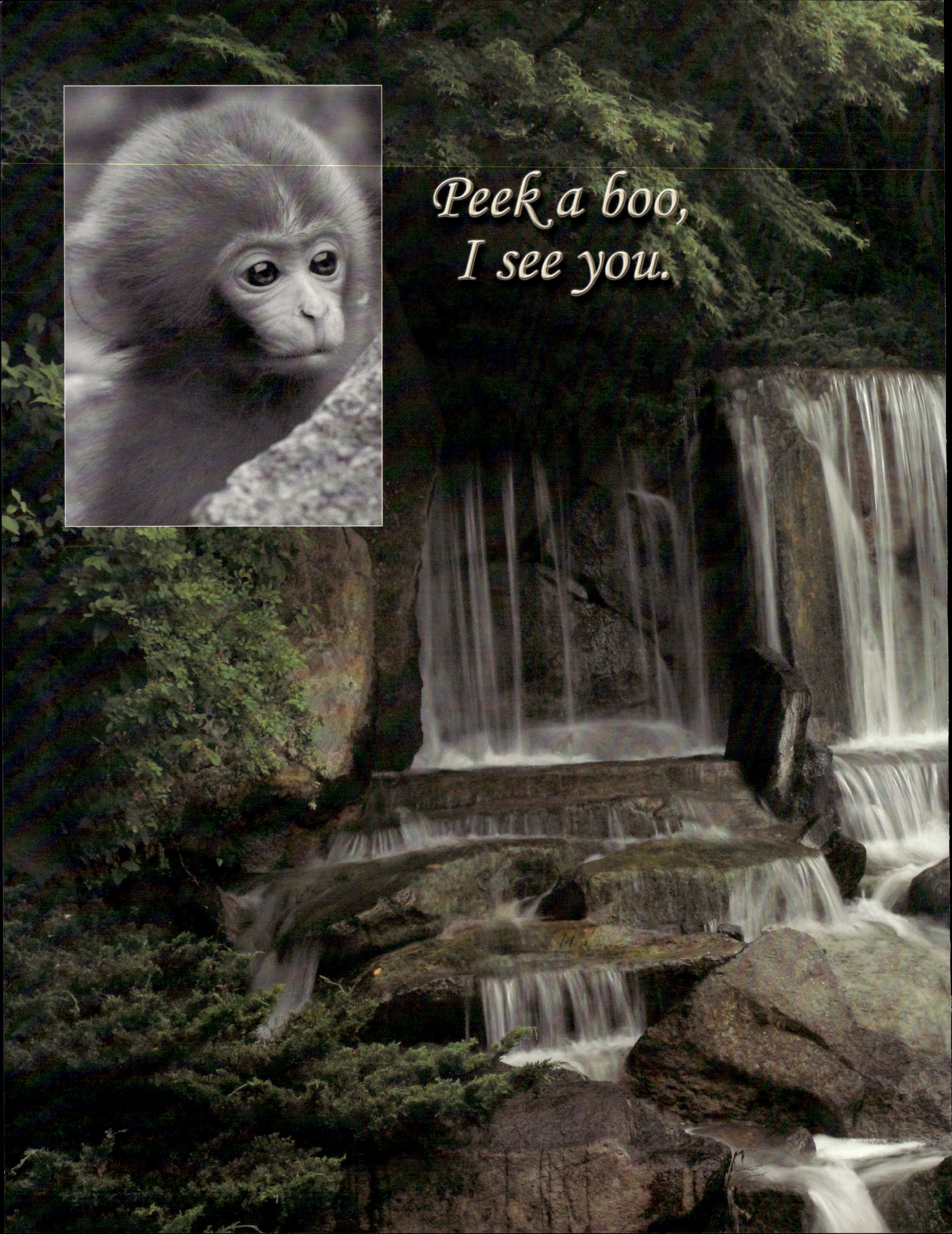

Peek a boo,
I see you.

I drink water and milk,
but not soda or beer.

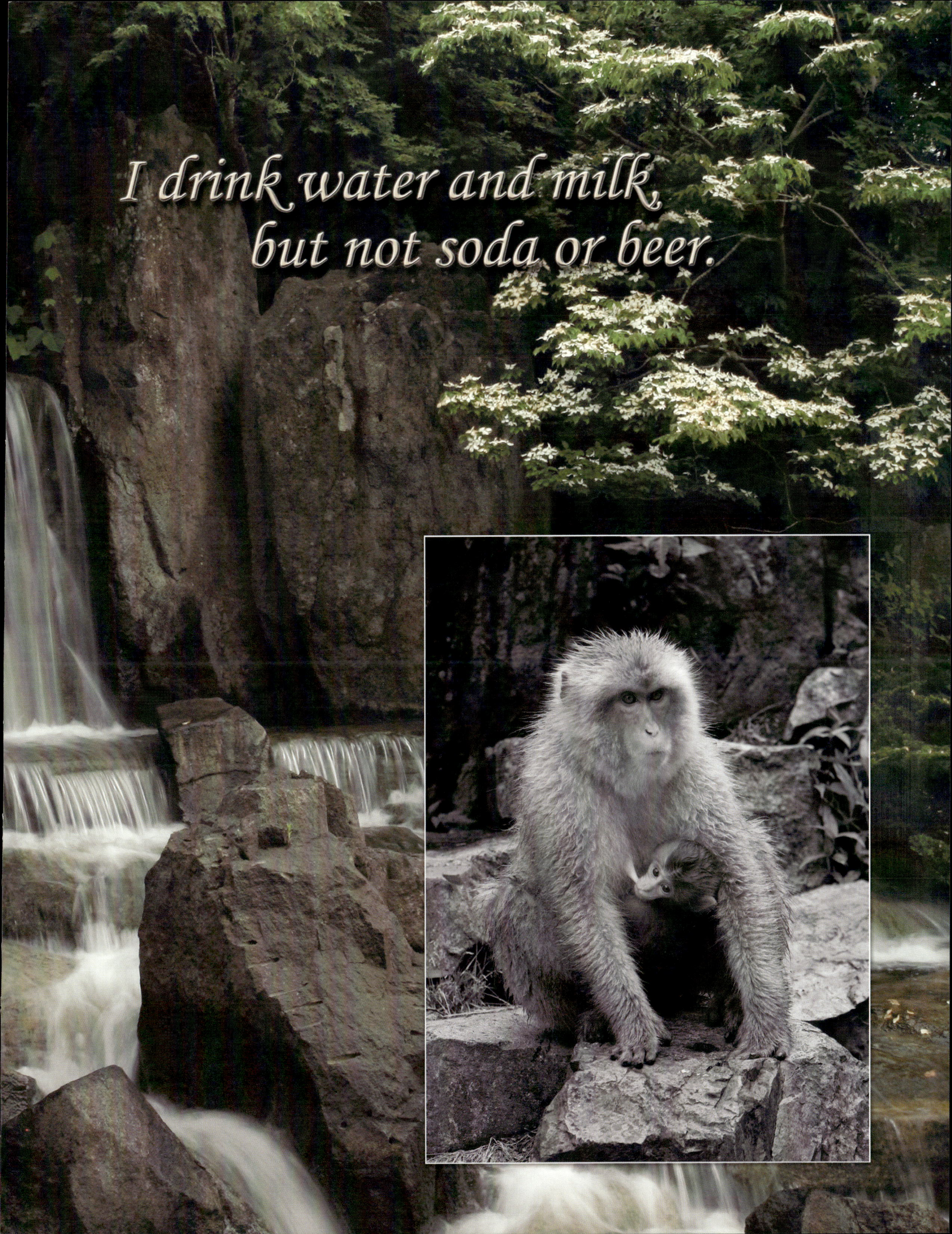

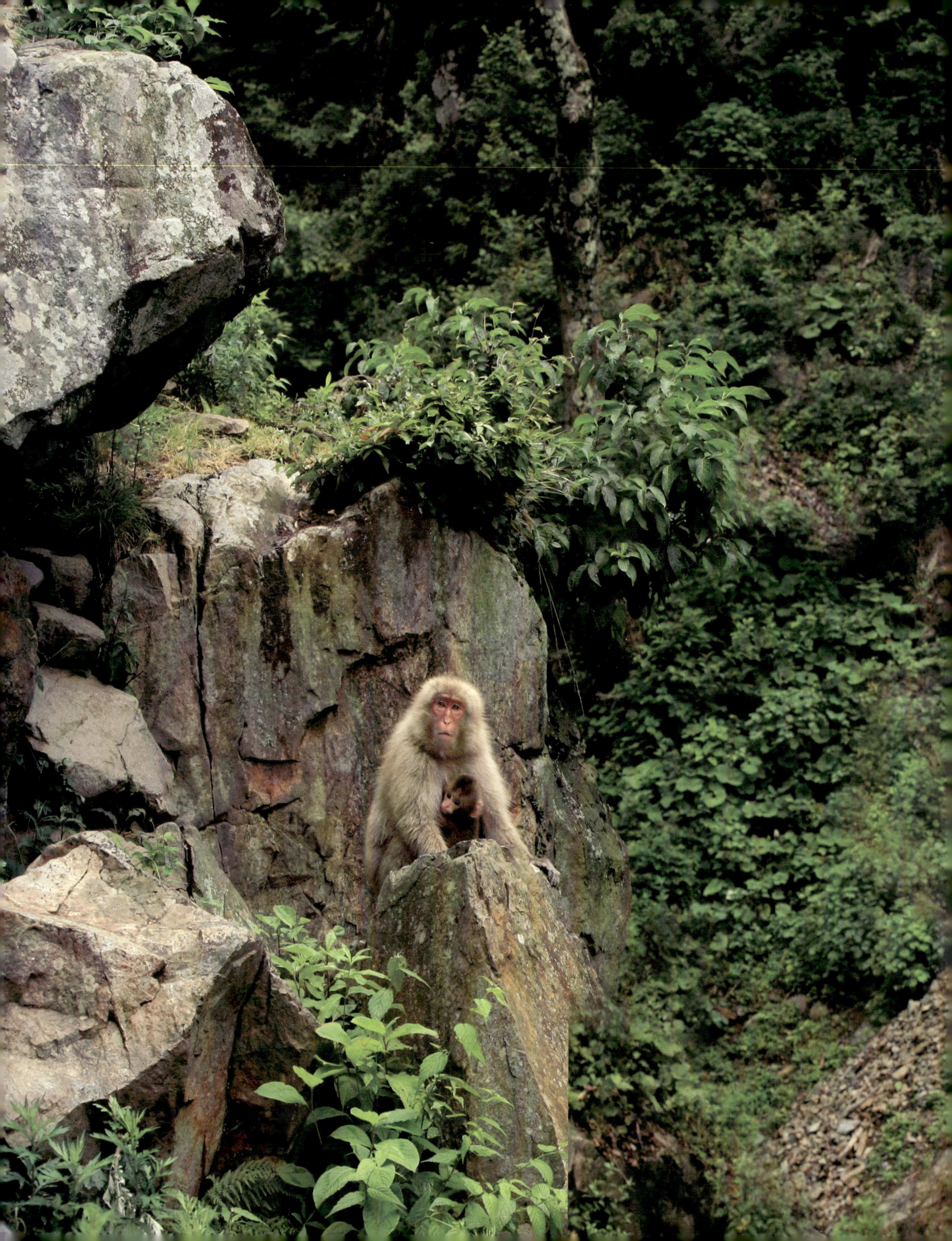

I stay close to my mom,
to be safe from harm.

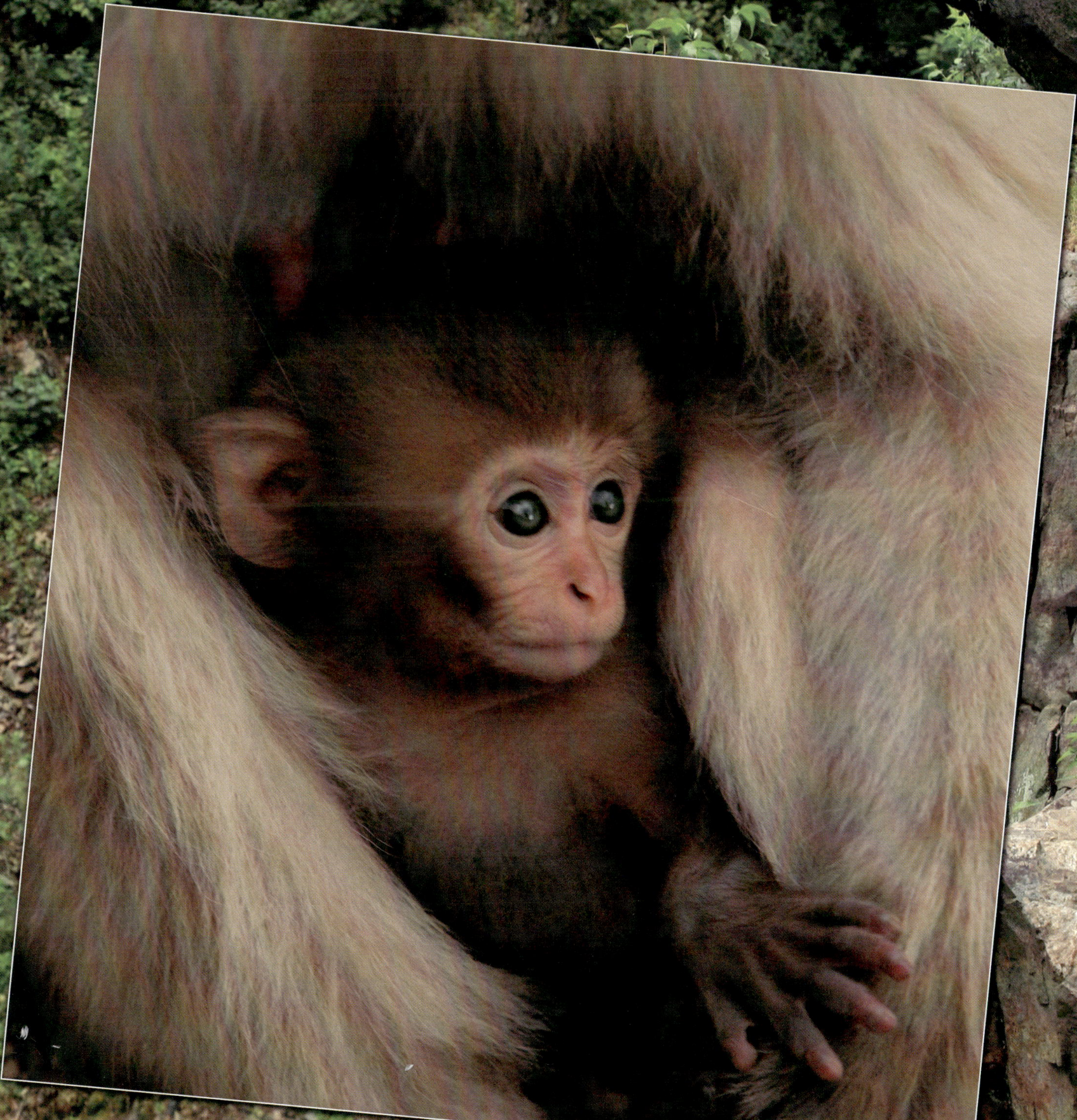

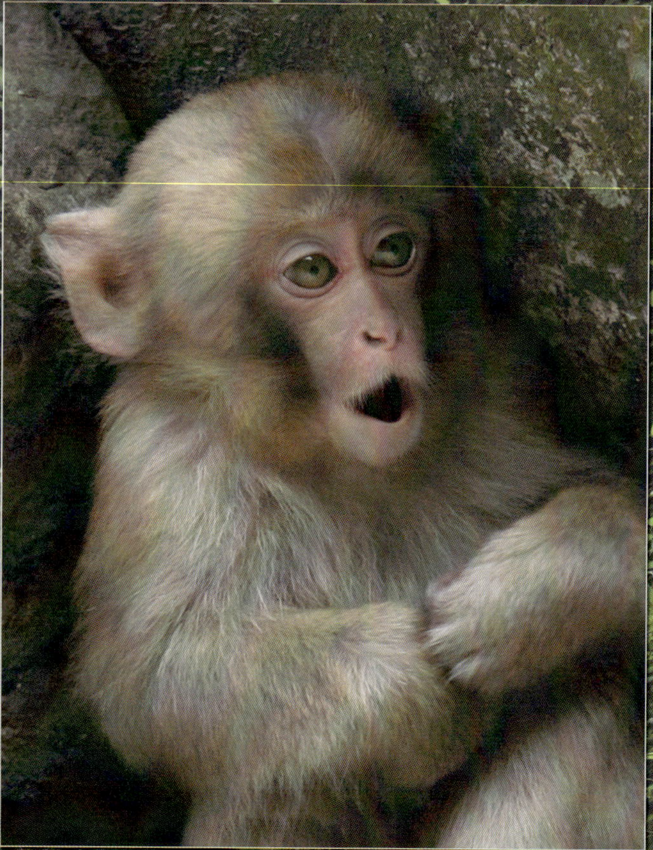

We have secret hiding places to hide from ...

... our enemies; fox , weasels, badgers, martens, racoon dogs, and bear.

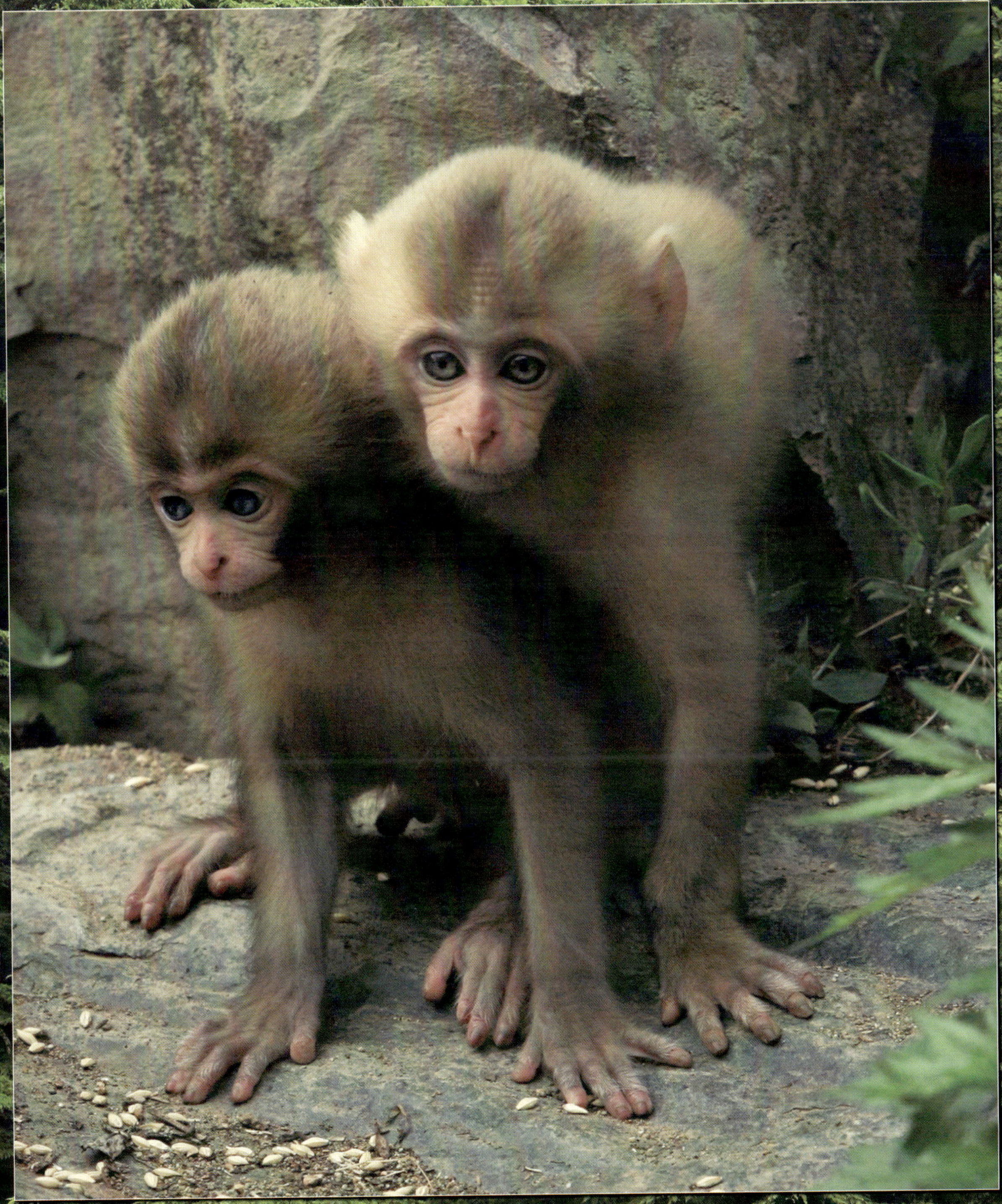

My friends are playing a game called twister.

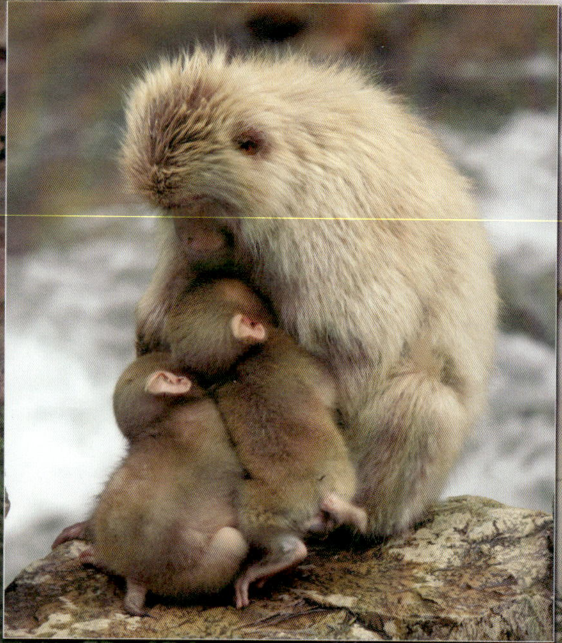

This milk
tastes great.

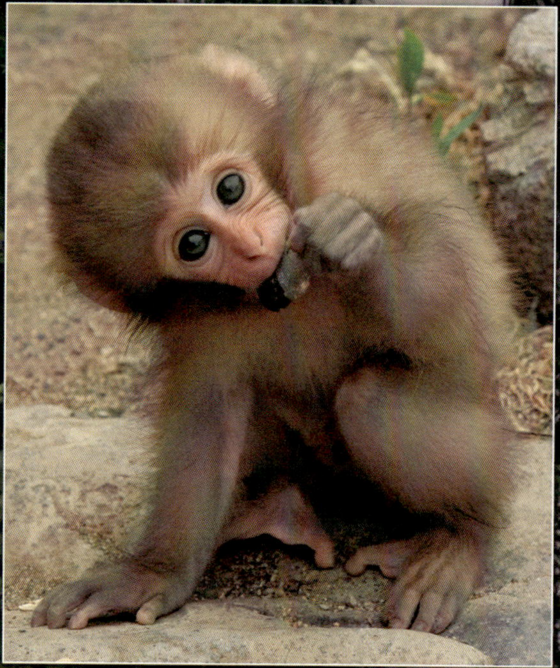

This rock
does not
taste good.

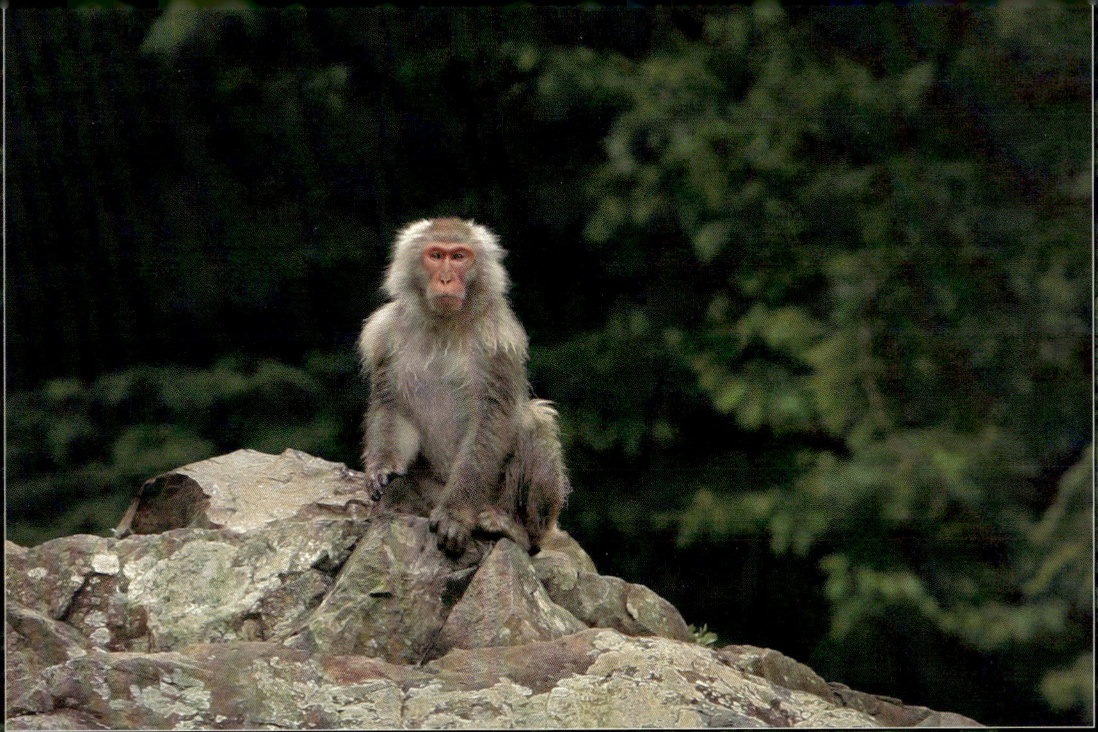

This guy eats healthy,
he is an athlete (football player).

Just kidding

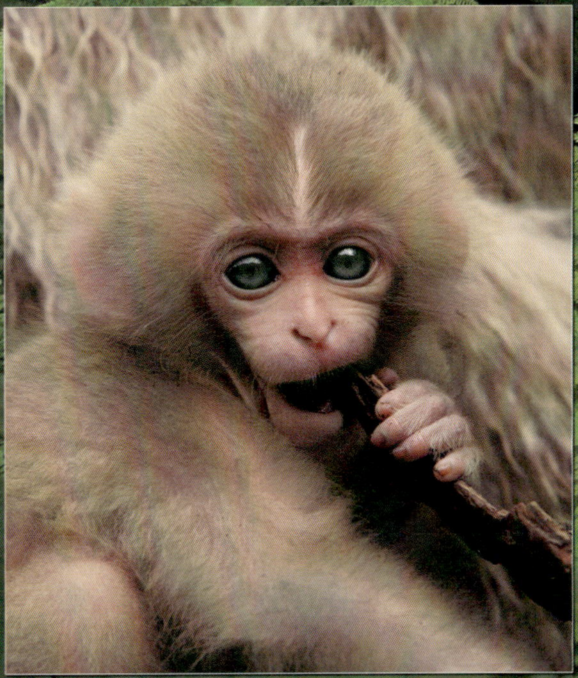

This stick does not
taste much better!

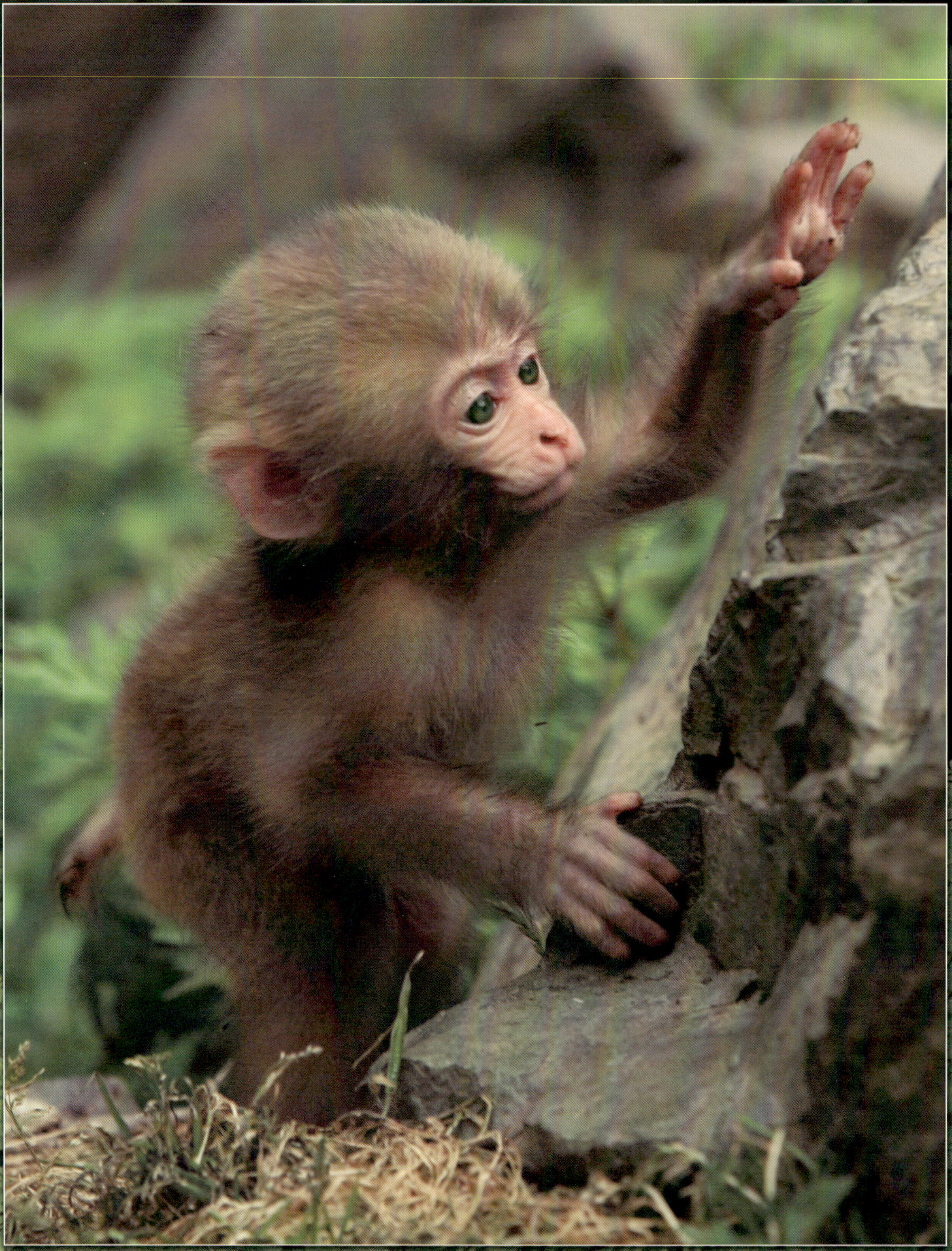

Even at the young age of 1 month, I am learning to climb

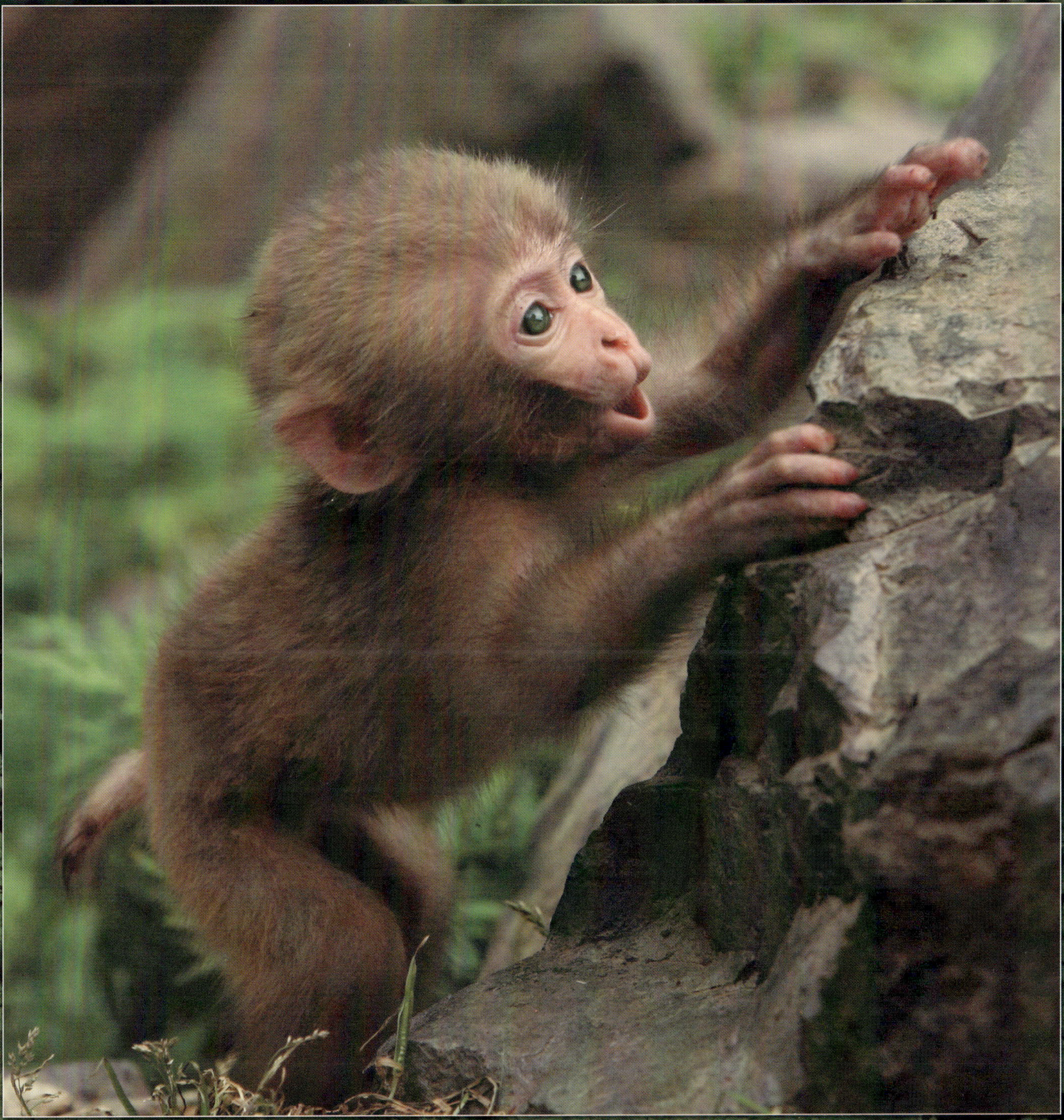

Could you climb at 1 month?

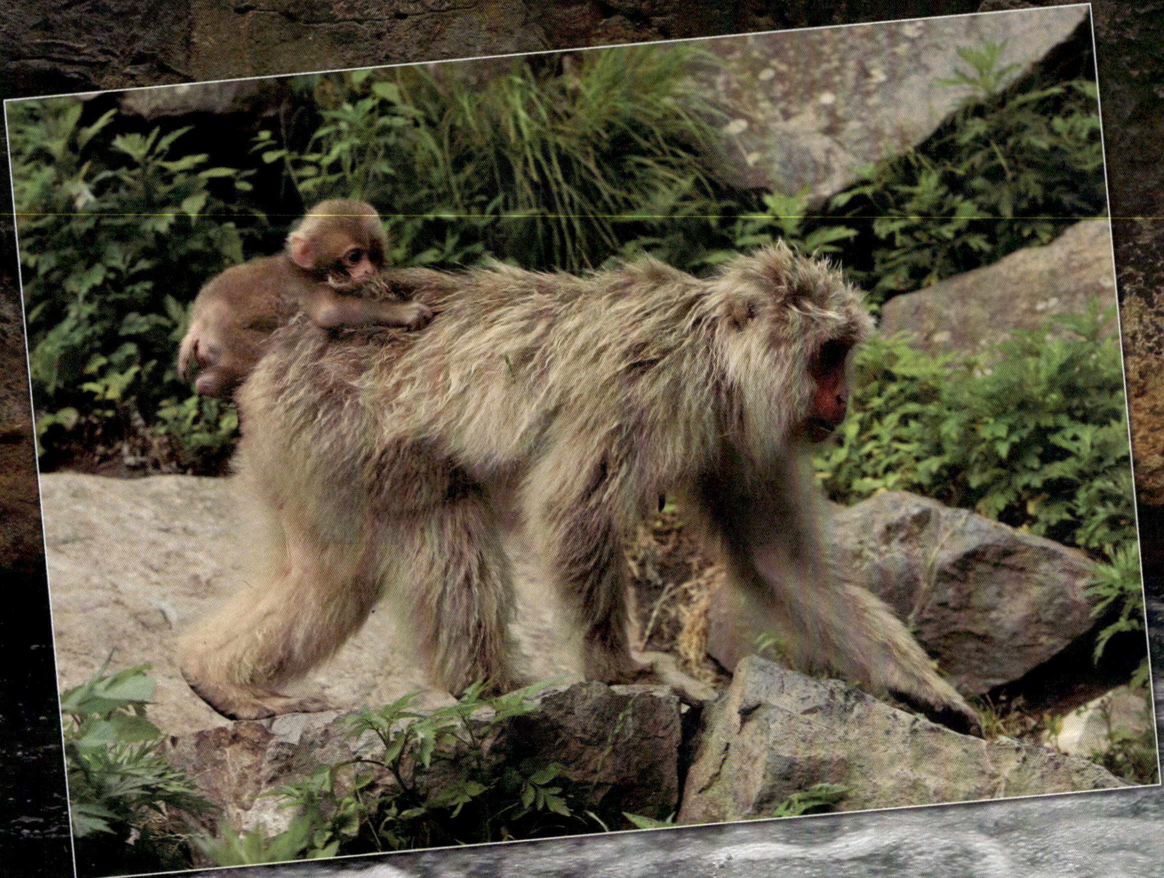

Neptune is barely "hanging on".

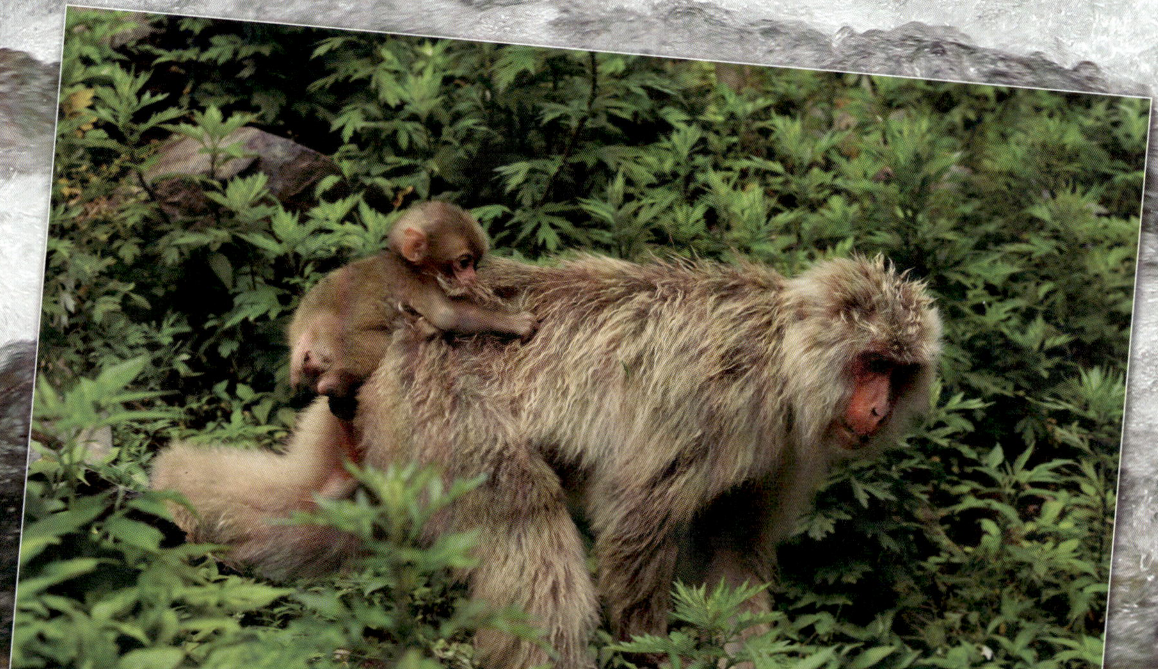

Humans ride bikes, cars, buses.
airplanes, trains, and subways.

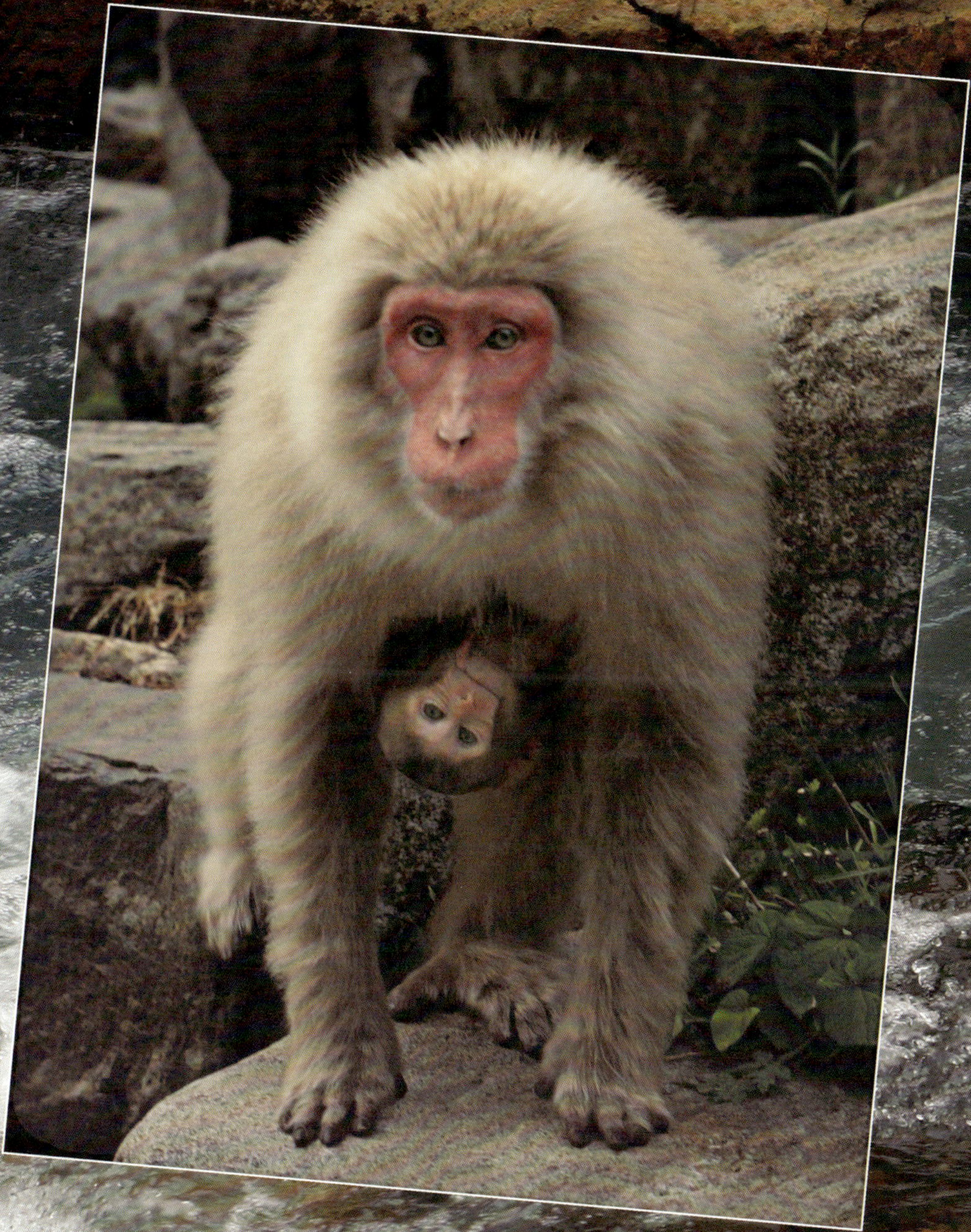

Monkeys ride their moms.

Can you find, where we are:
1) telling secrets, 2) wrestling,
3) snacking, 4) playing leapfrog

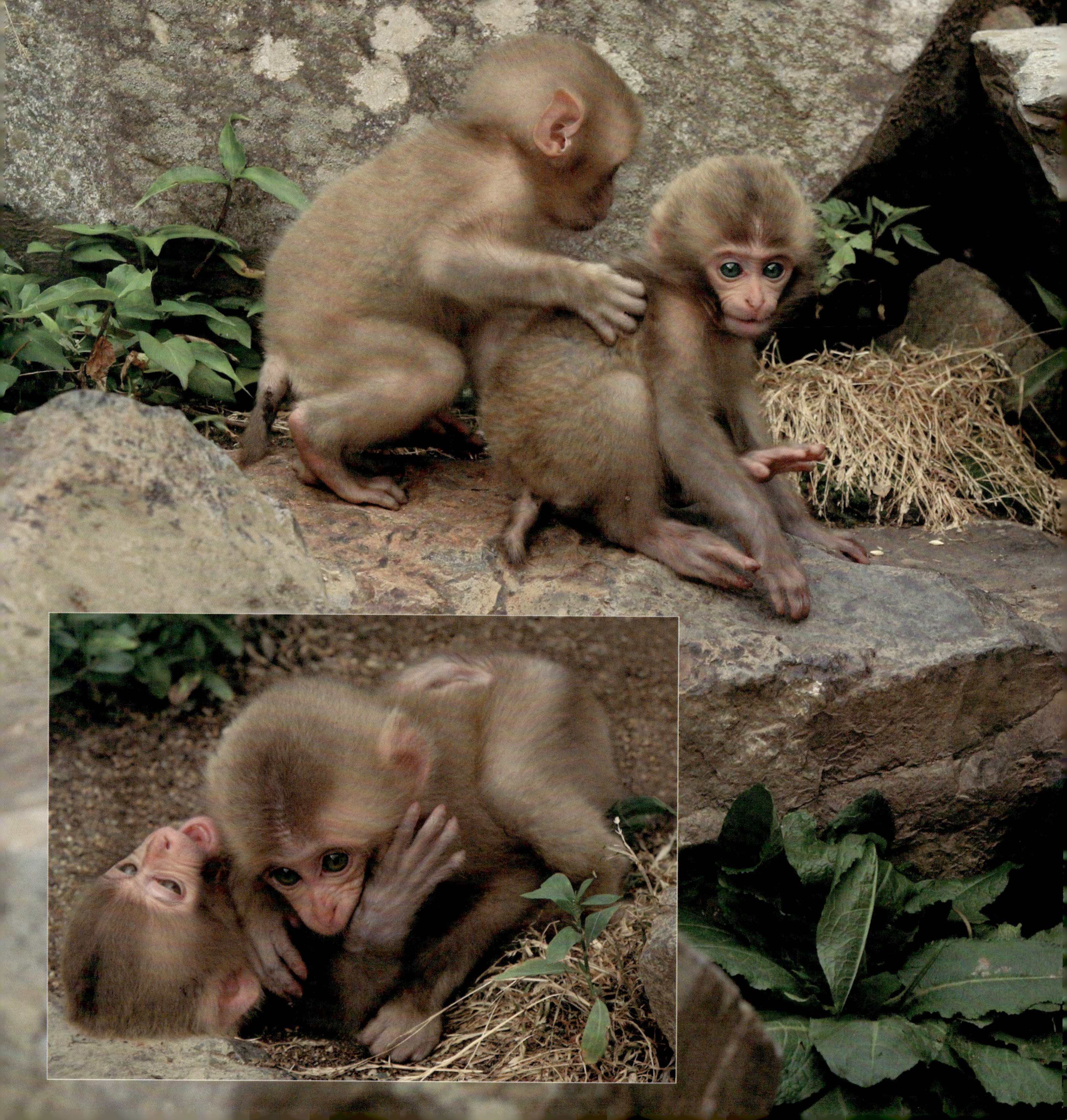

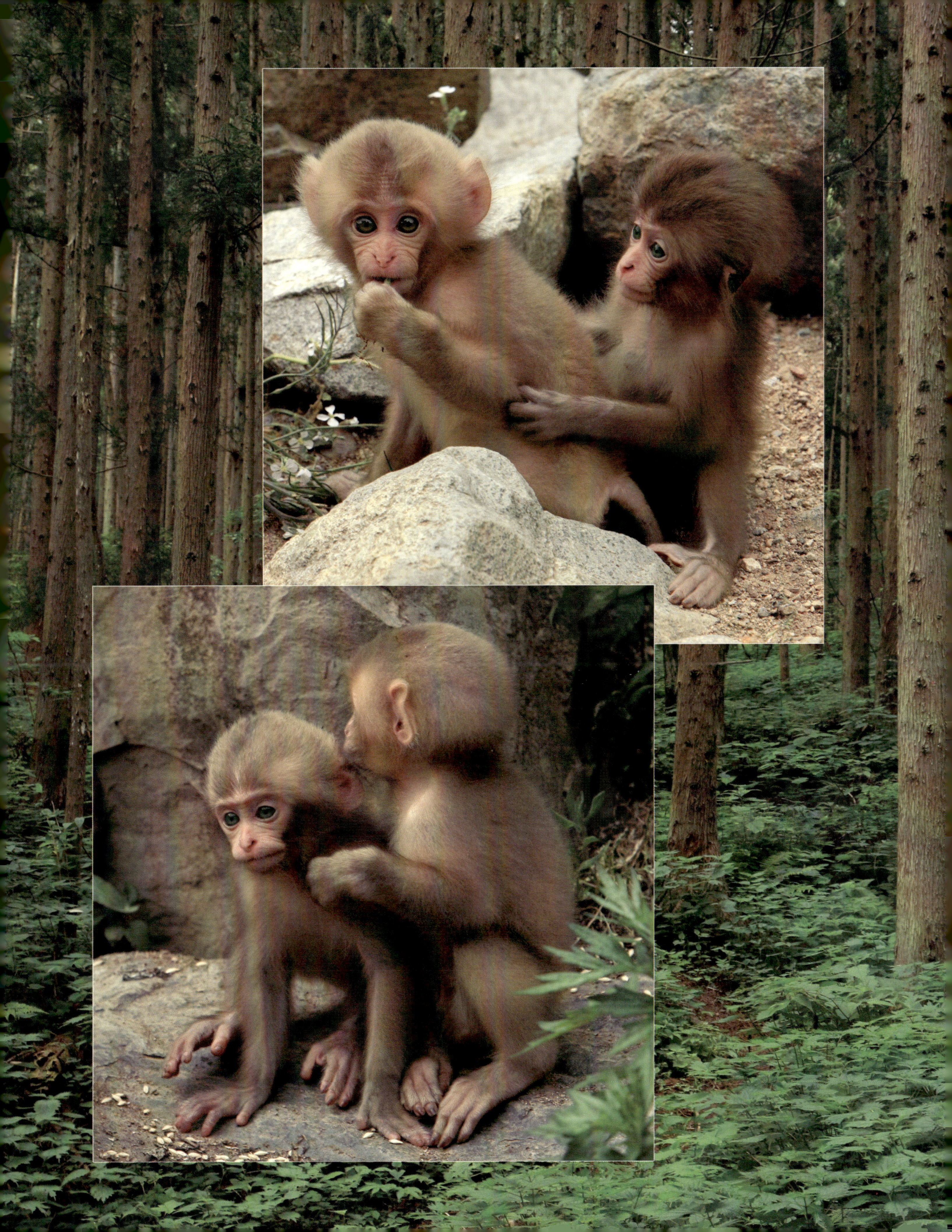

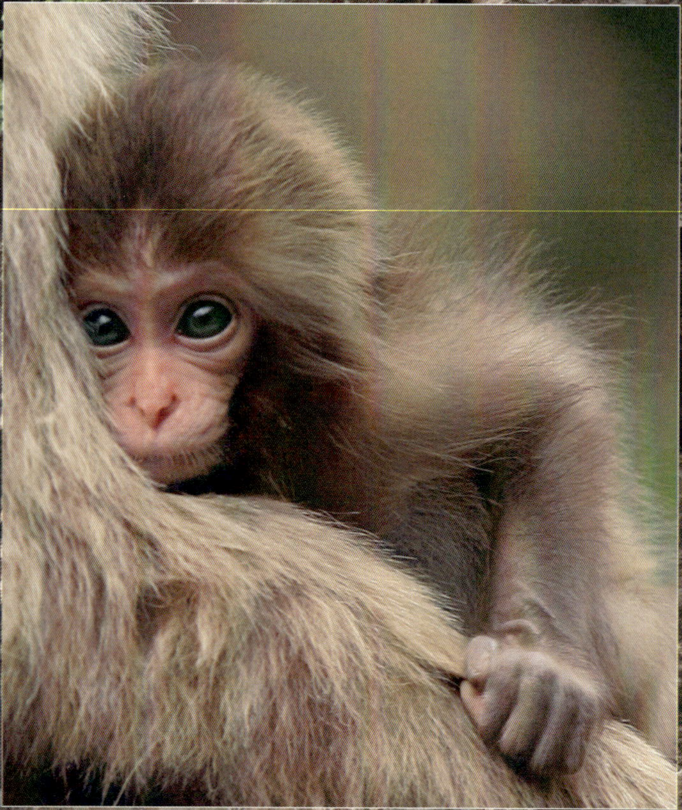

We are special animals that can grasp with our hands and feet.

Can you grasp with your feet?

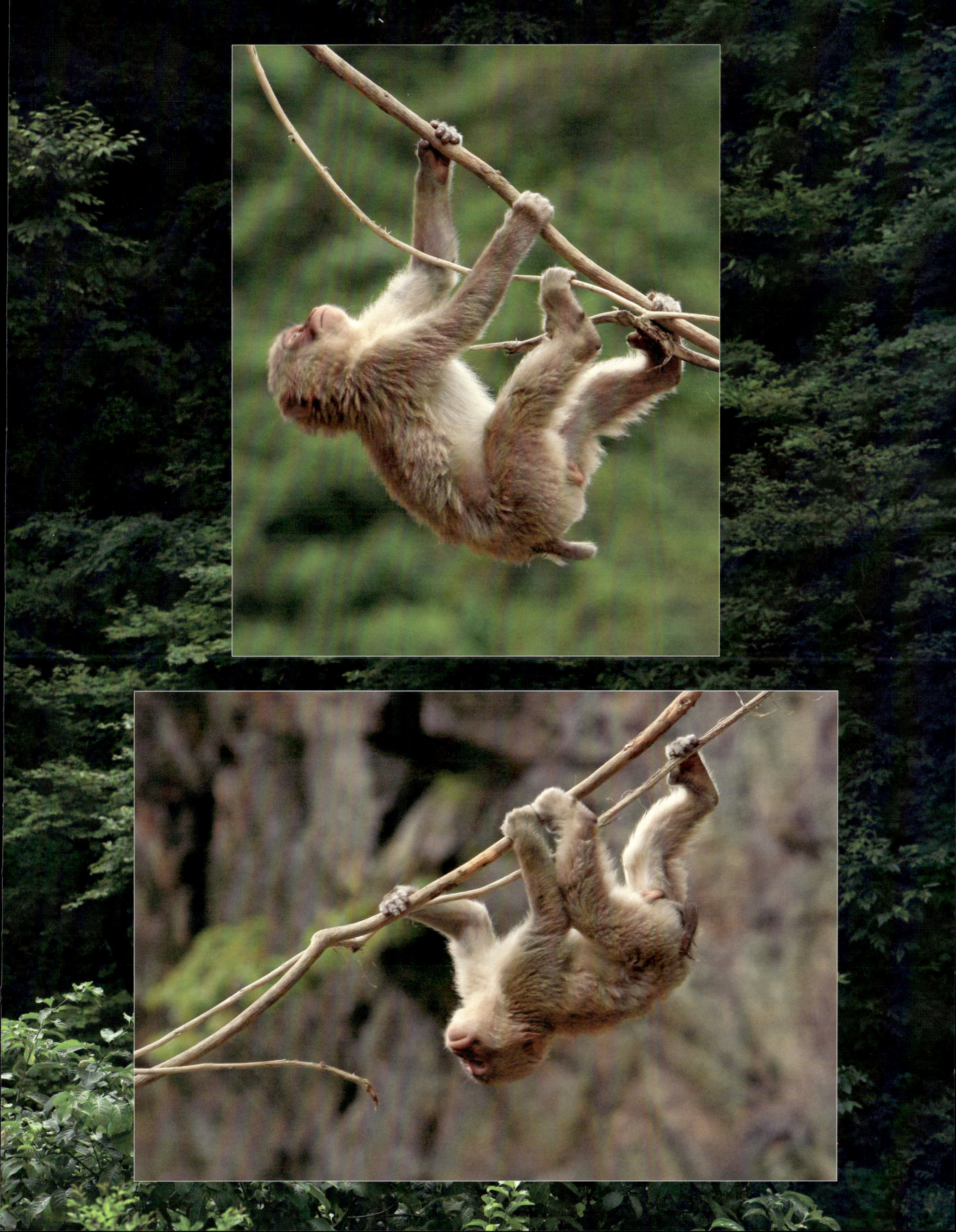

My monkey troop has 200 monkeys.

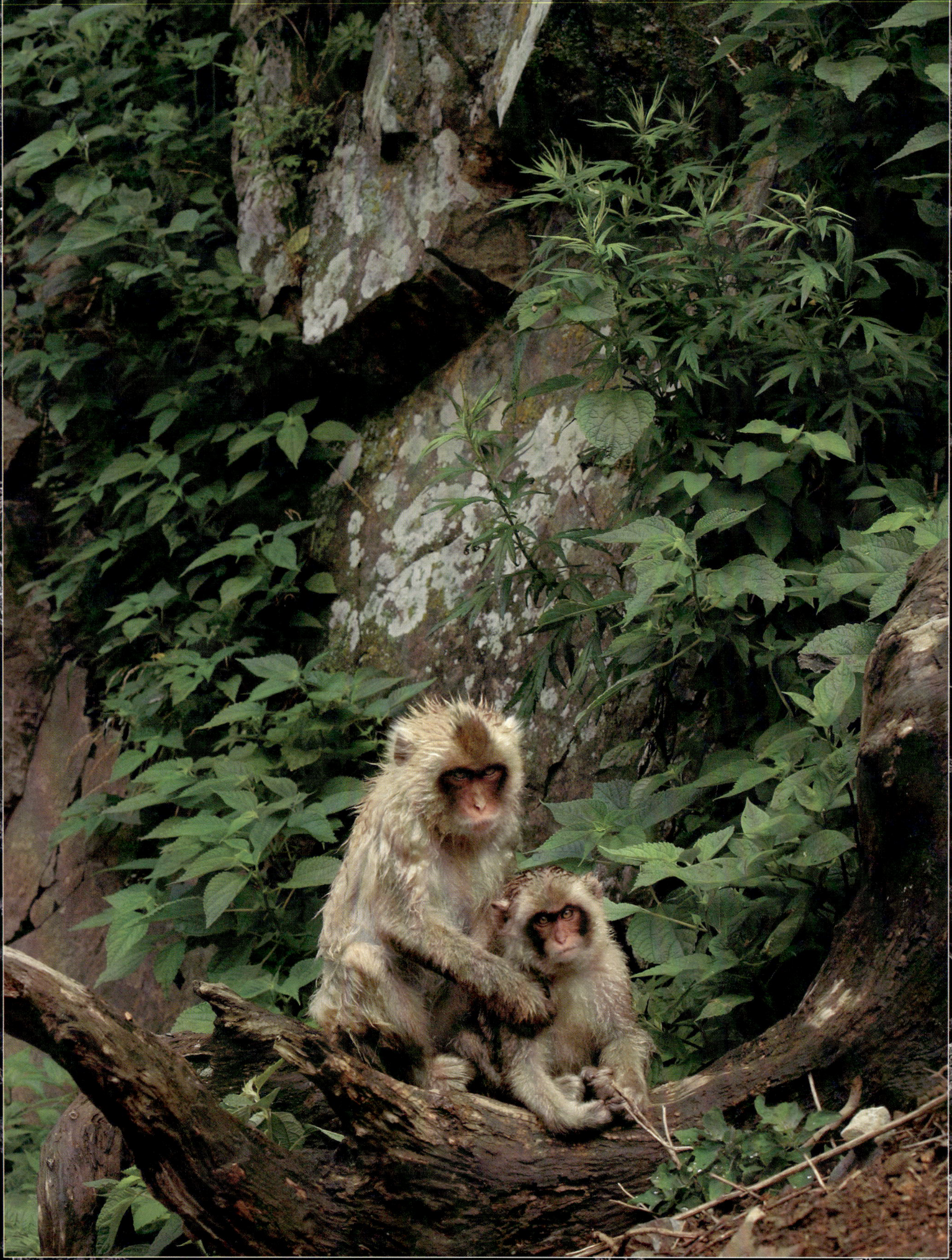

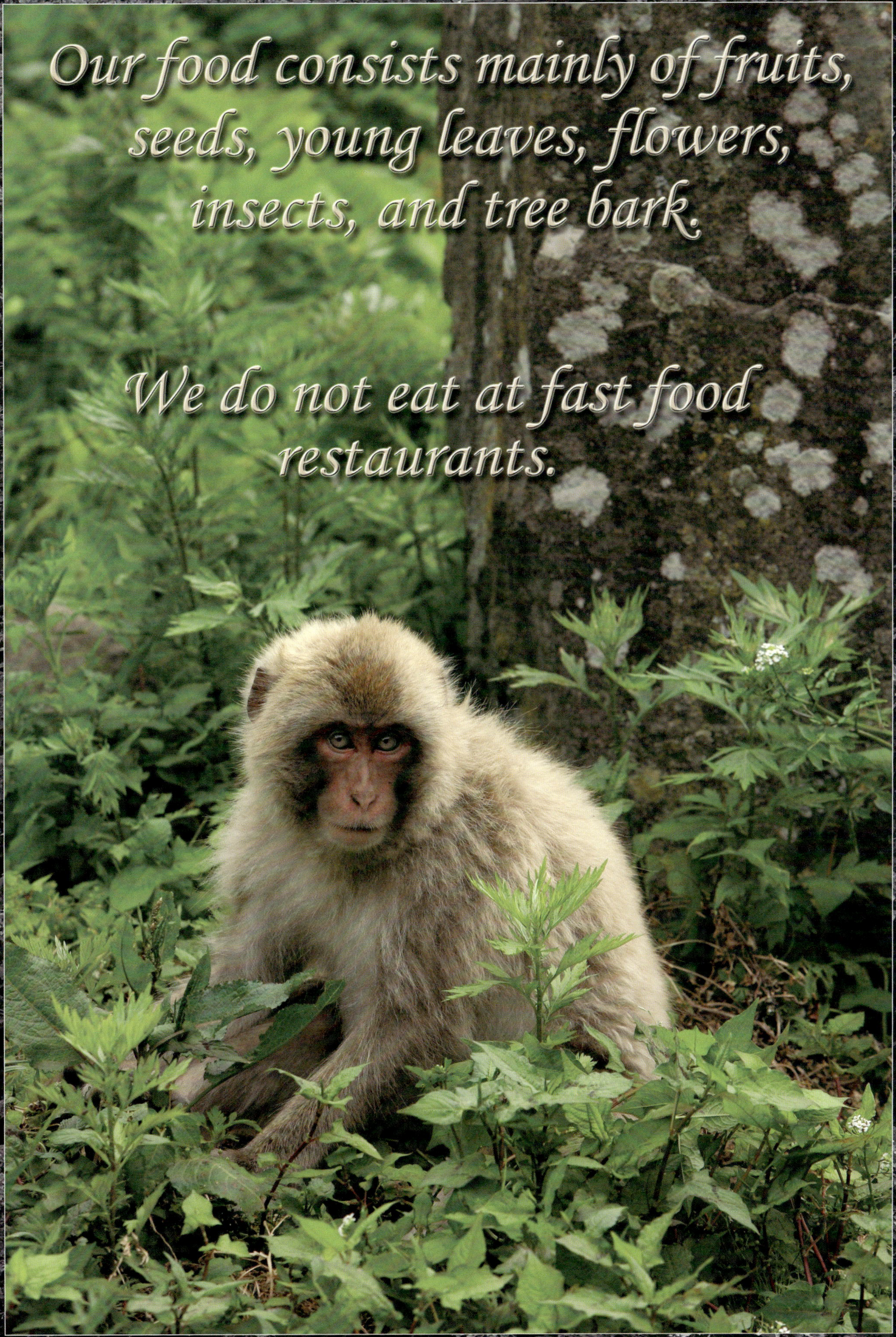
Our food consists mainly of fruits, seeds, young leaves, flowers, insects, and tree bark.
We do not eat at fast food restaurants.

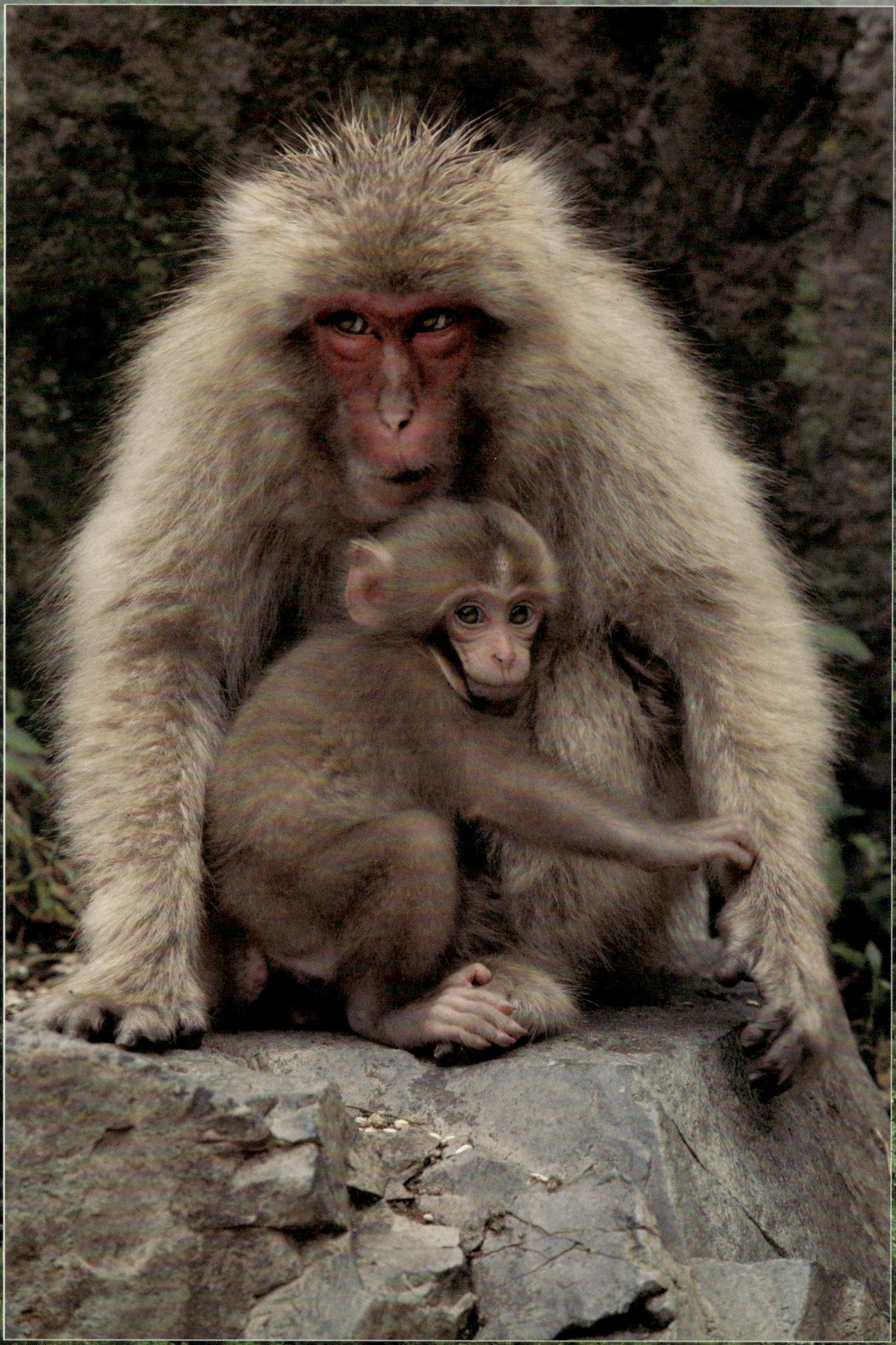

Don't mess with this dad!

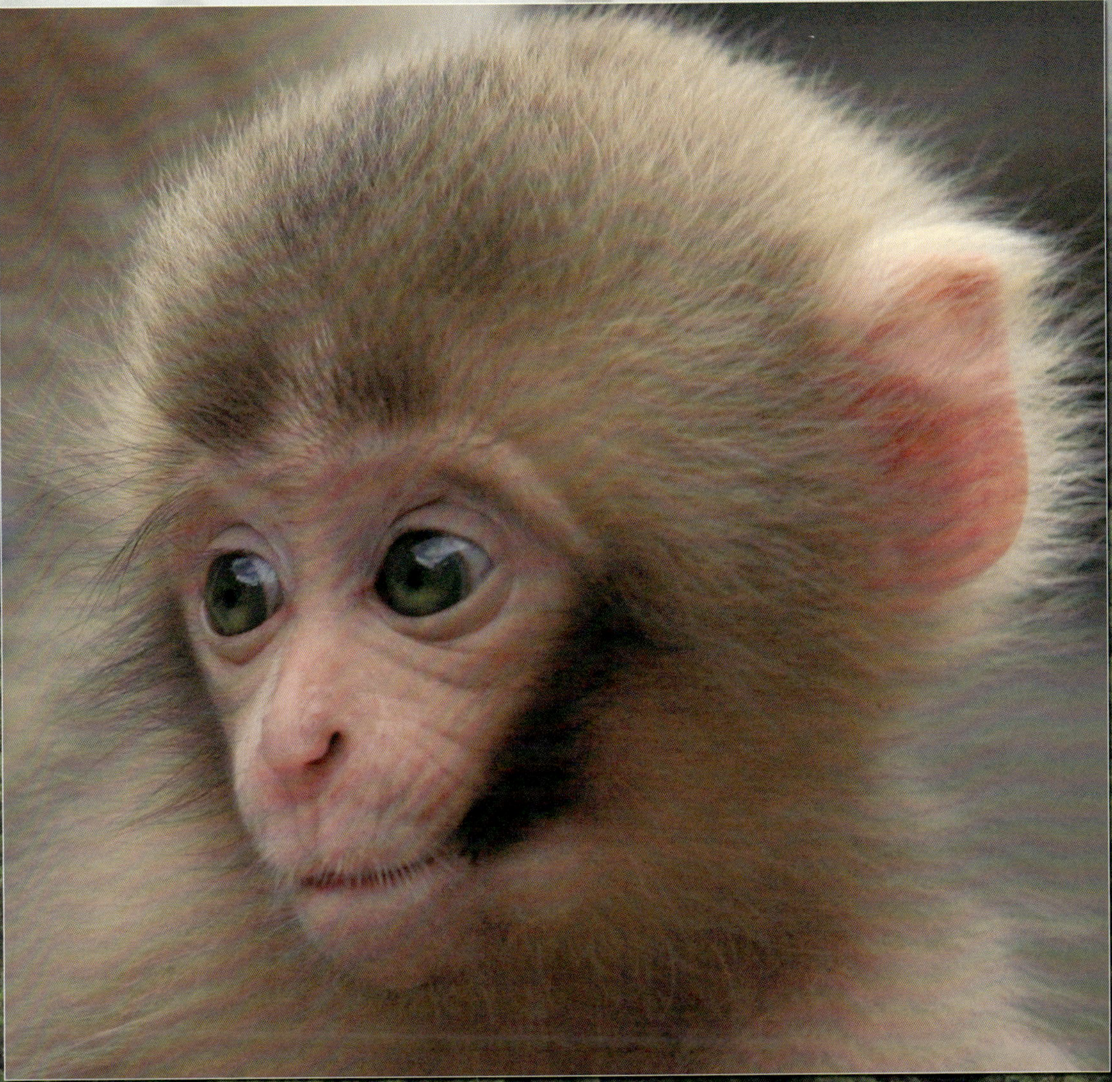

Cliffs can be dangerous.

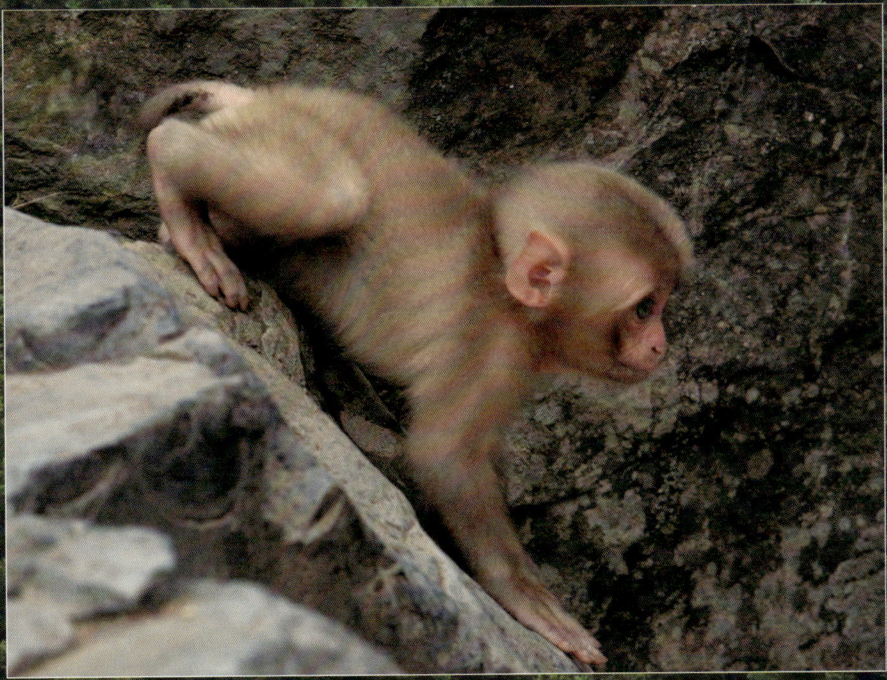

It is hard to climb ...

... but my mom is always

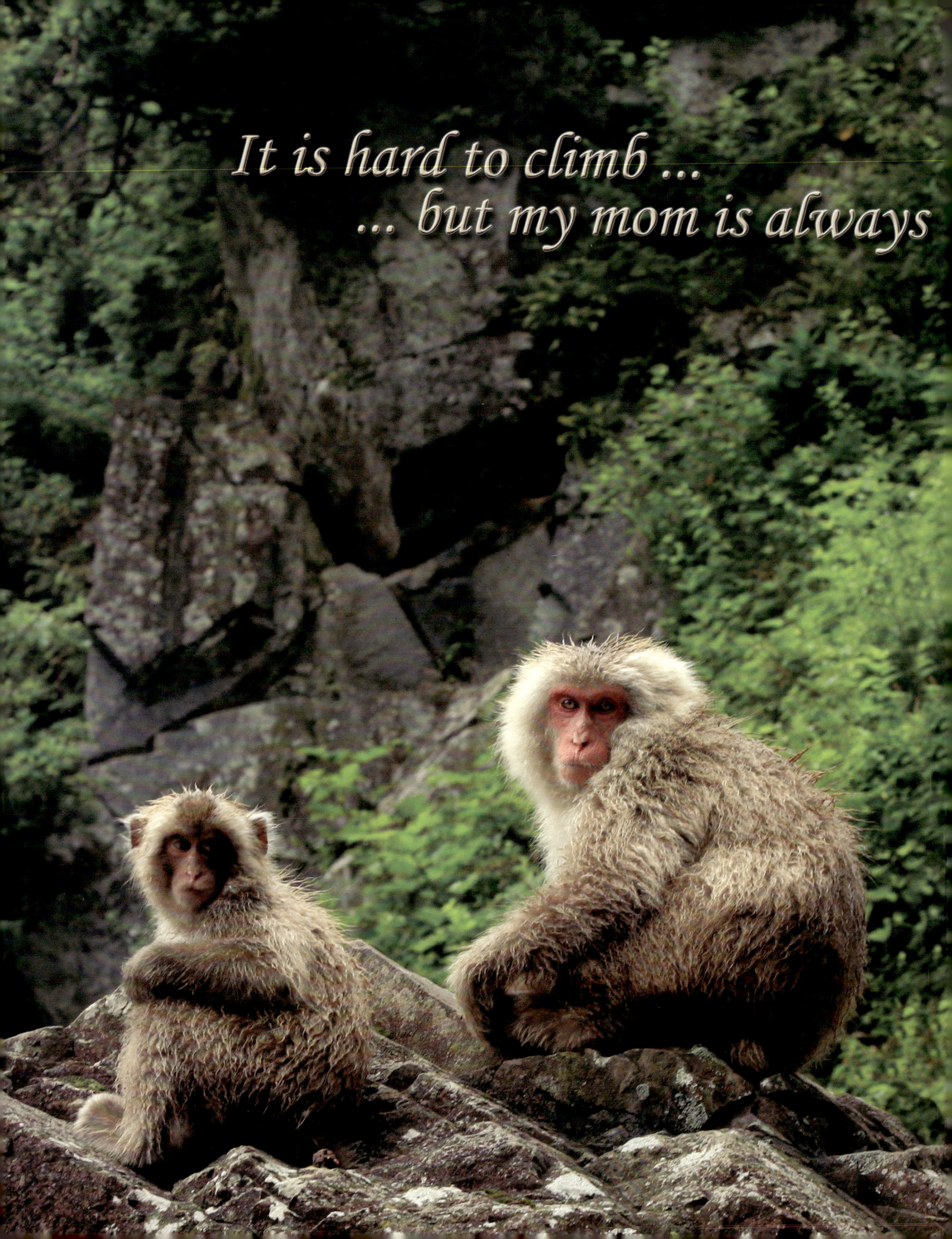

there to help.

"Hi Neptune".

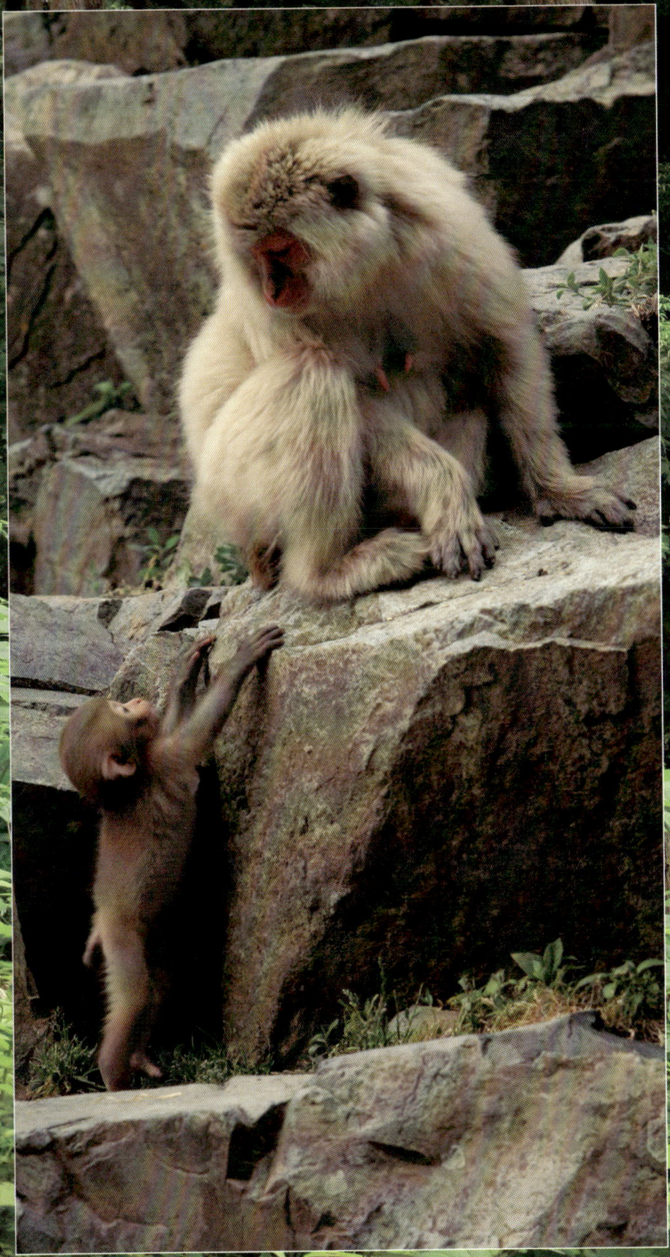

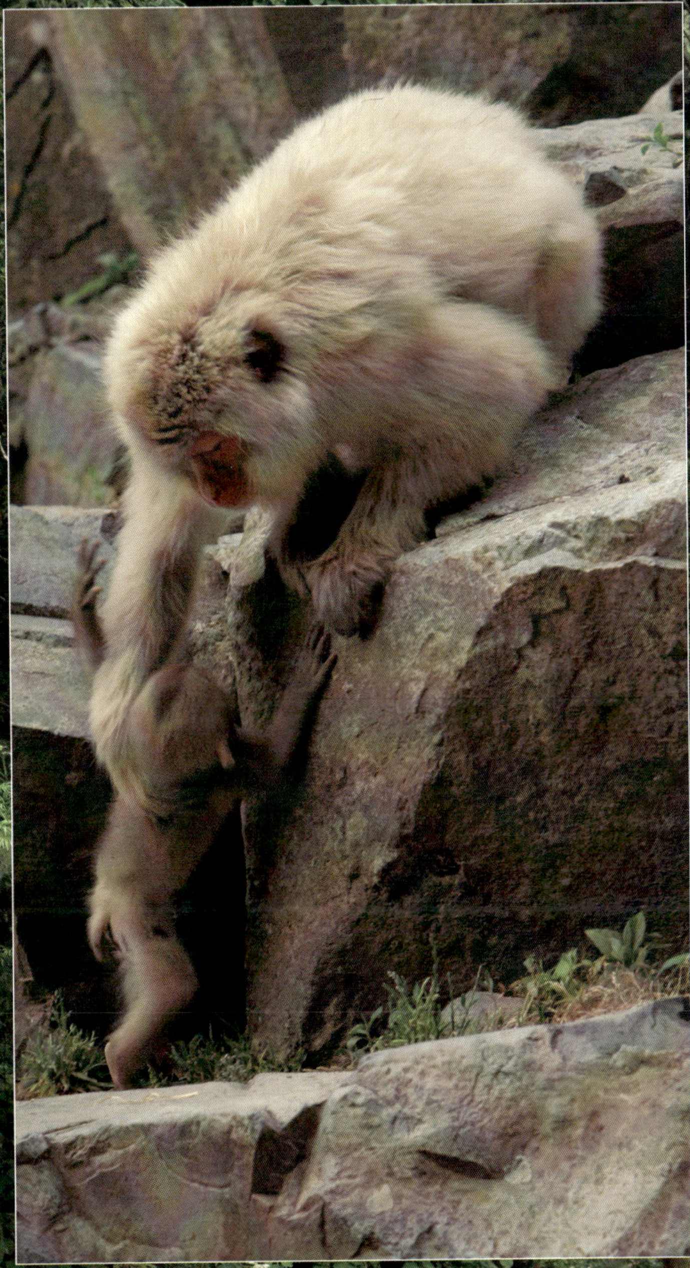

"I'll help you sweetie!"

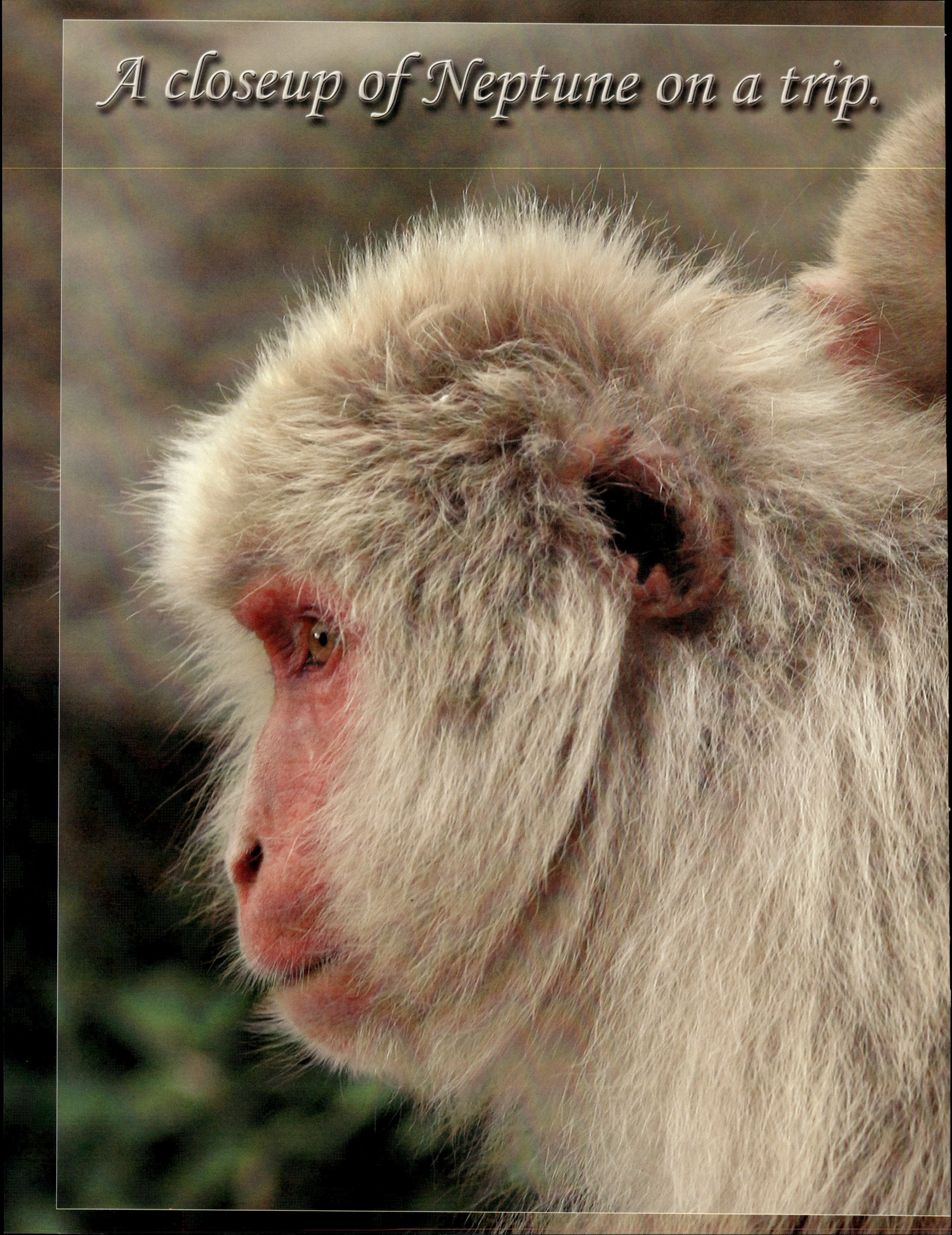

A closeup of Neptune on a trip.

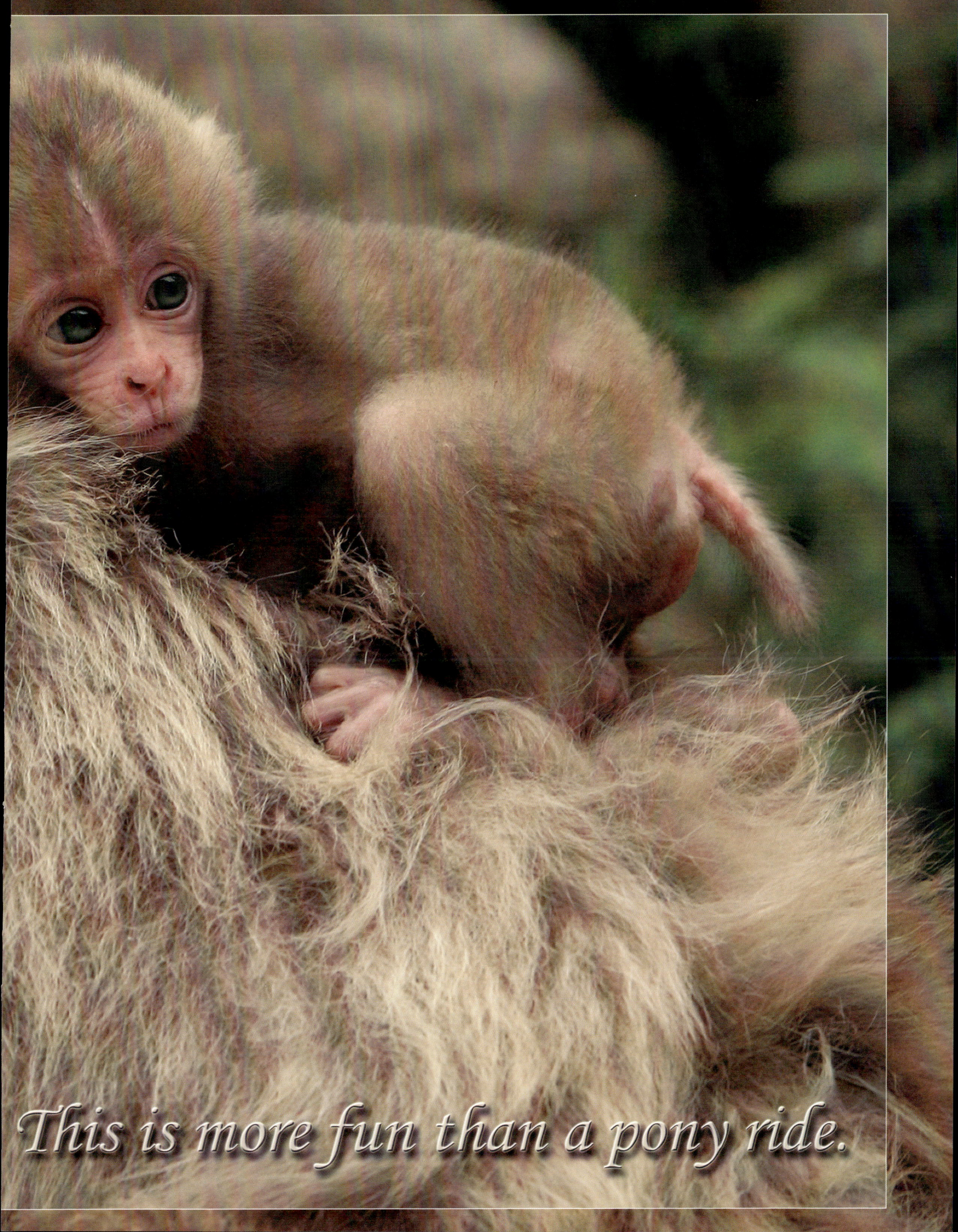

This is more fun than a pony ride.

This is a snow monkey way of showing who is in charge (the monkey on top).

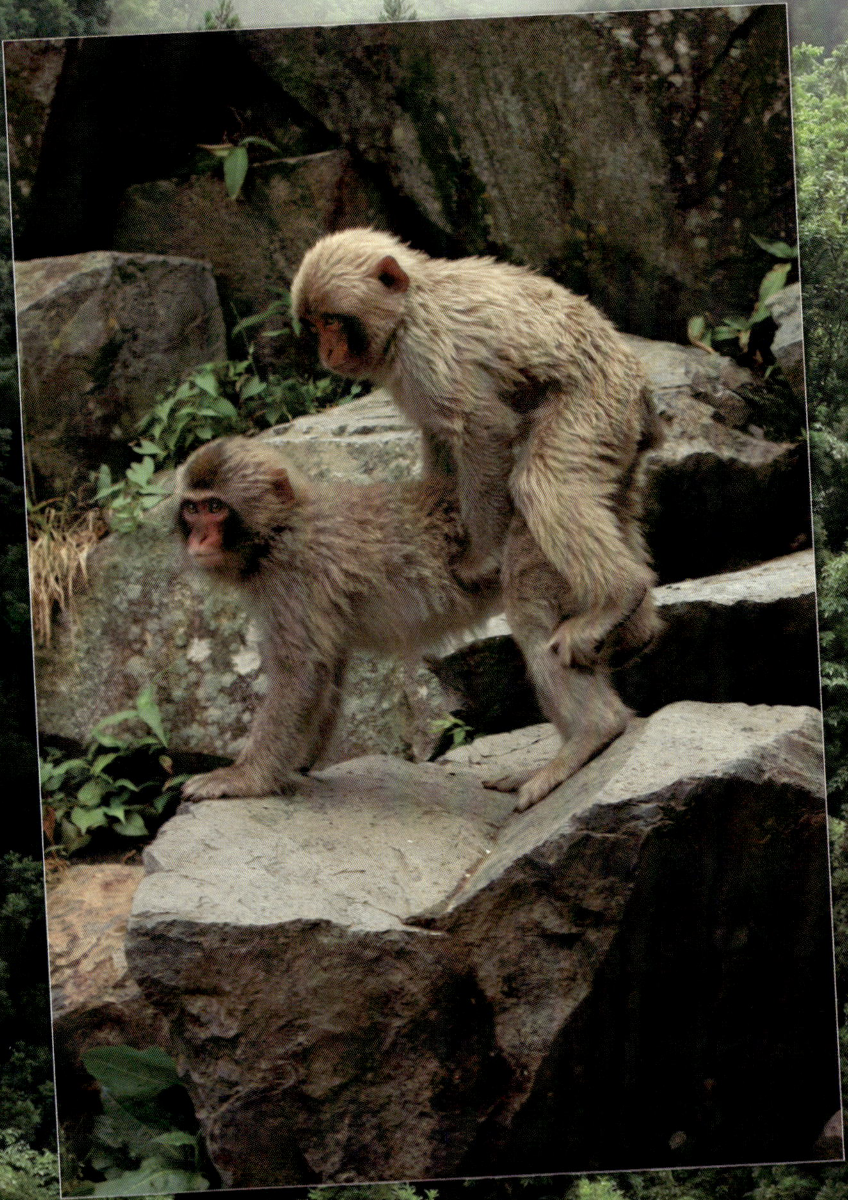

The bottom monkey will now allow the top monkey to eat first.

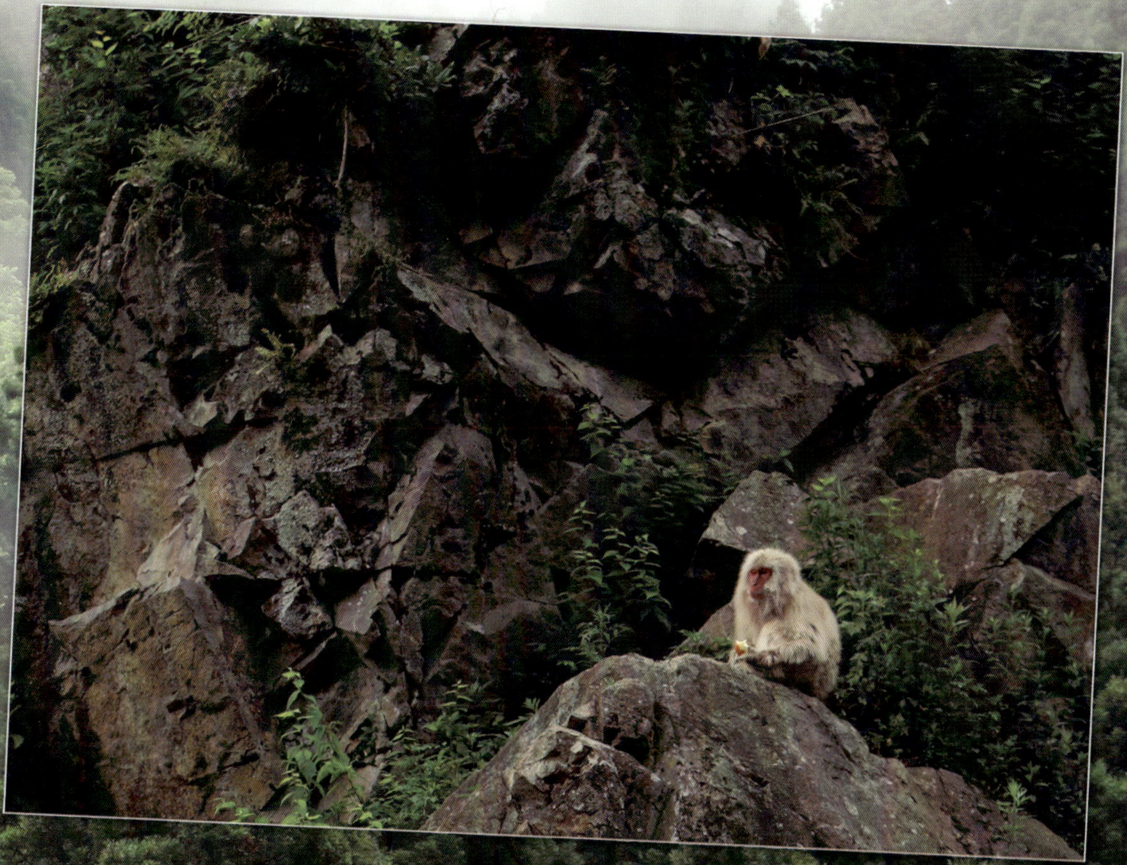

Have you ever teased someone or "pulled their leg?"

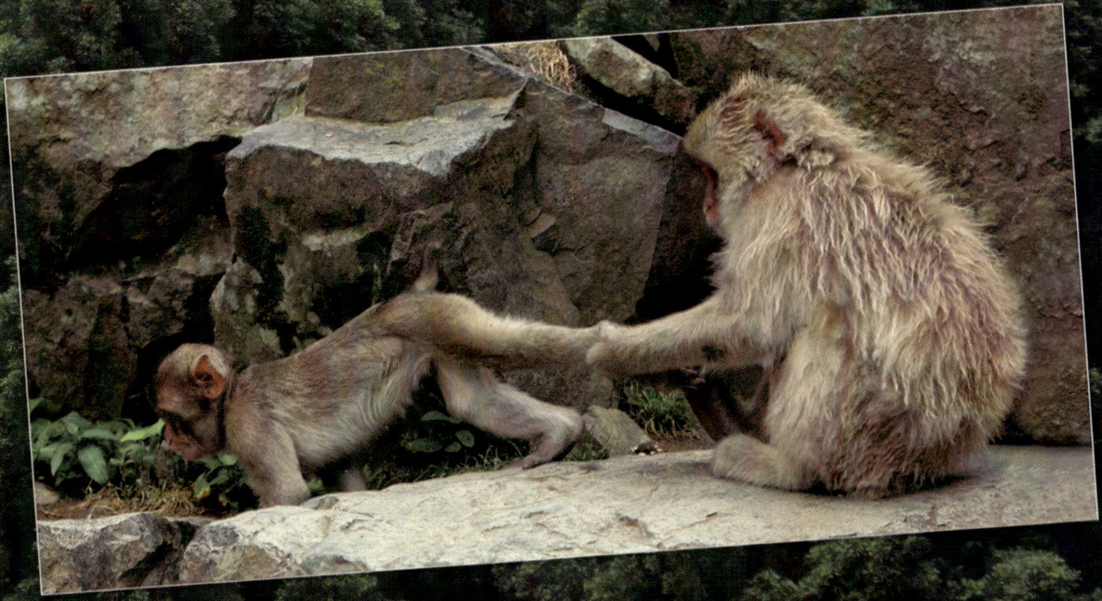

Before crossing the street ...

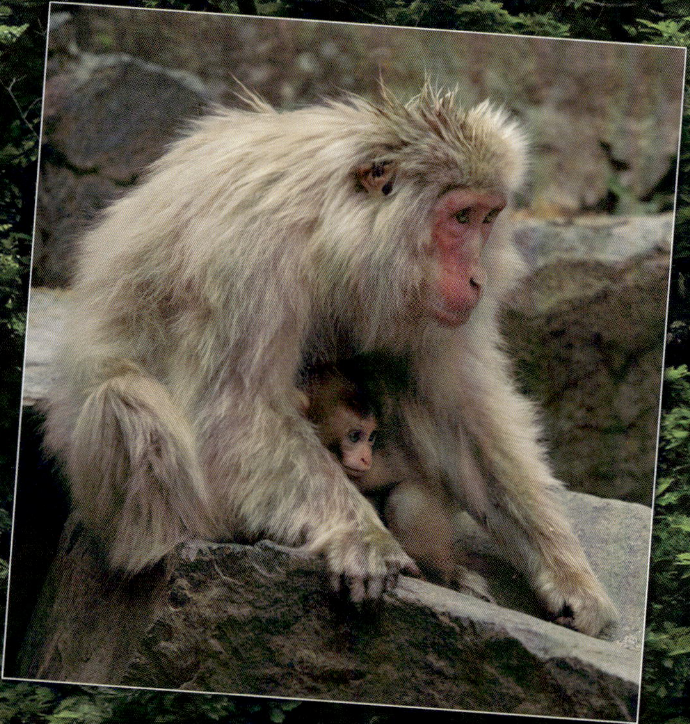

... look to the right,

and look to the left.

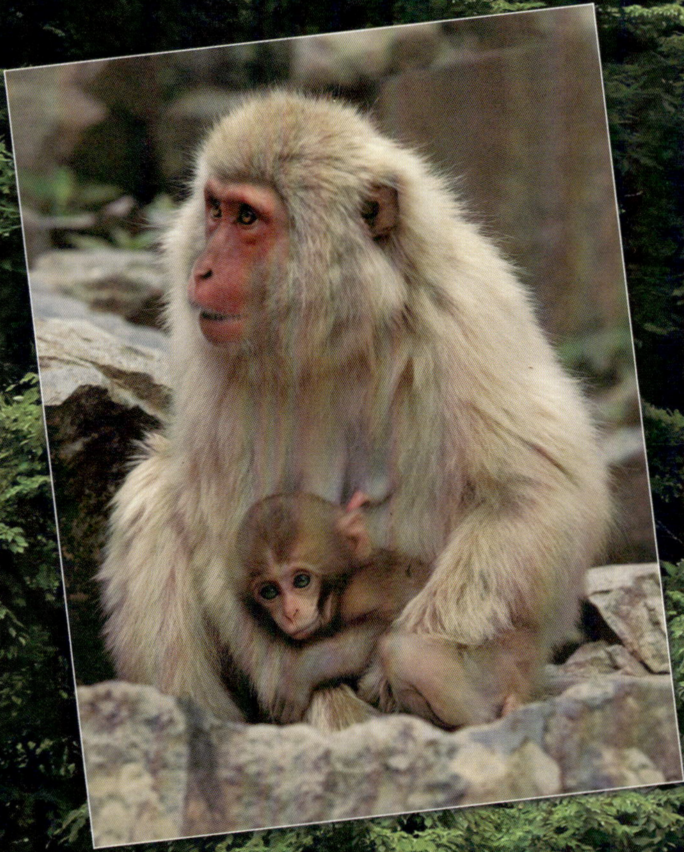

"Hang on" to mom,
if she walks or runs.

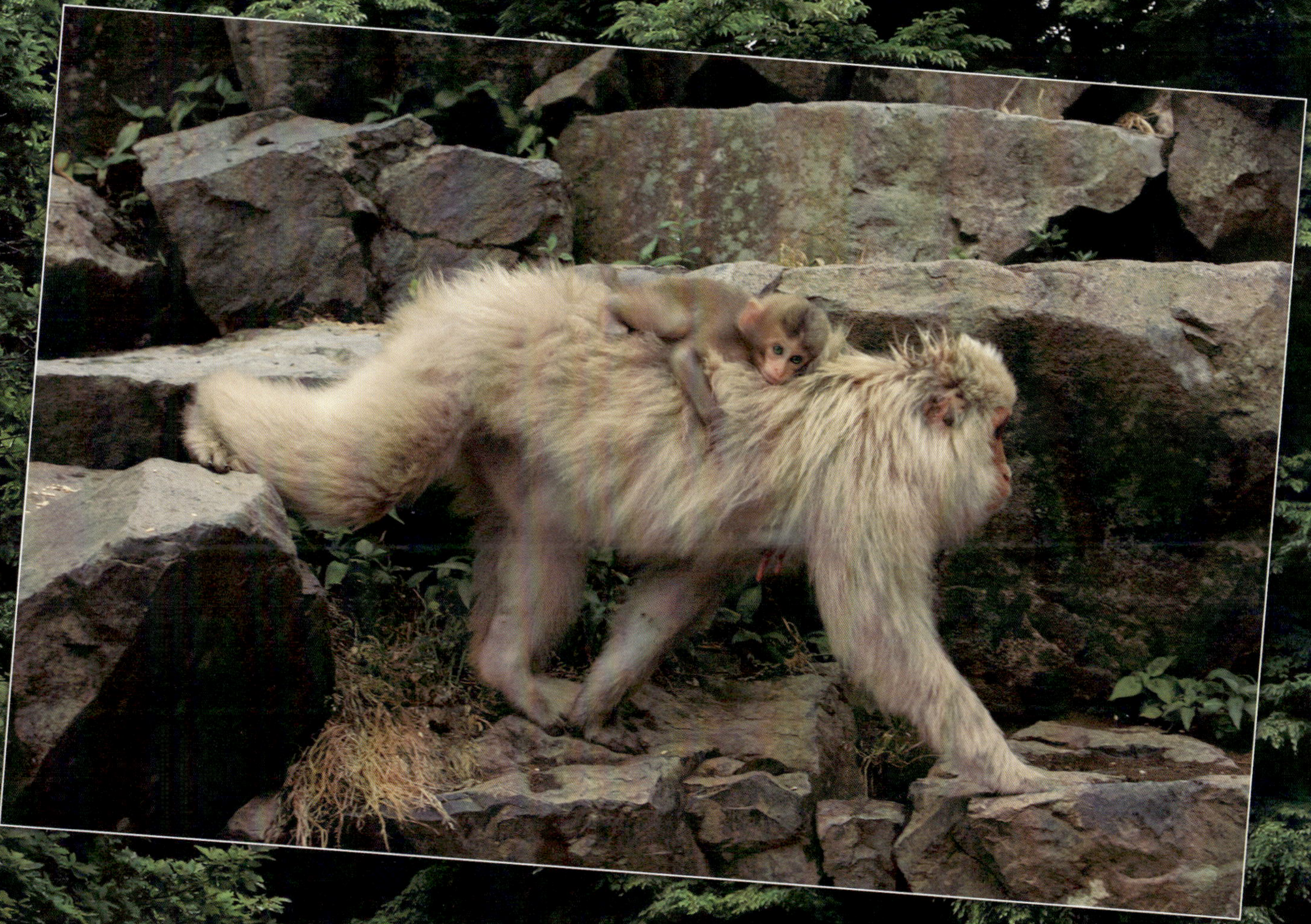

"Hang on Neptune!"

I sure am thirsty.

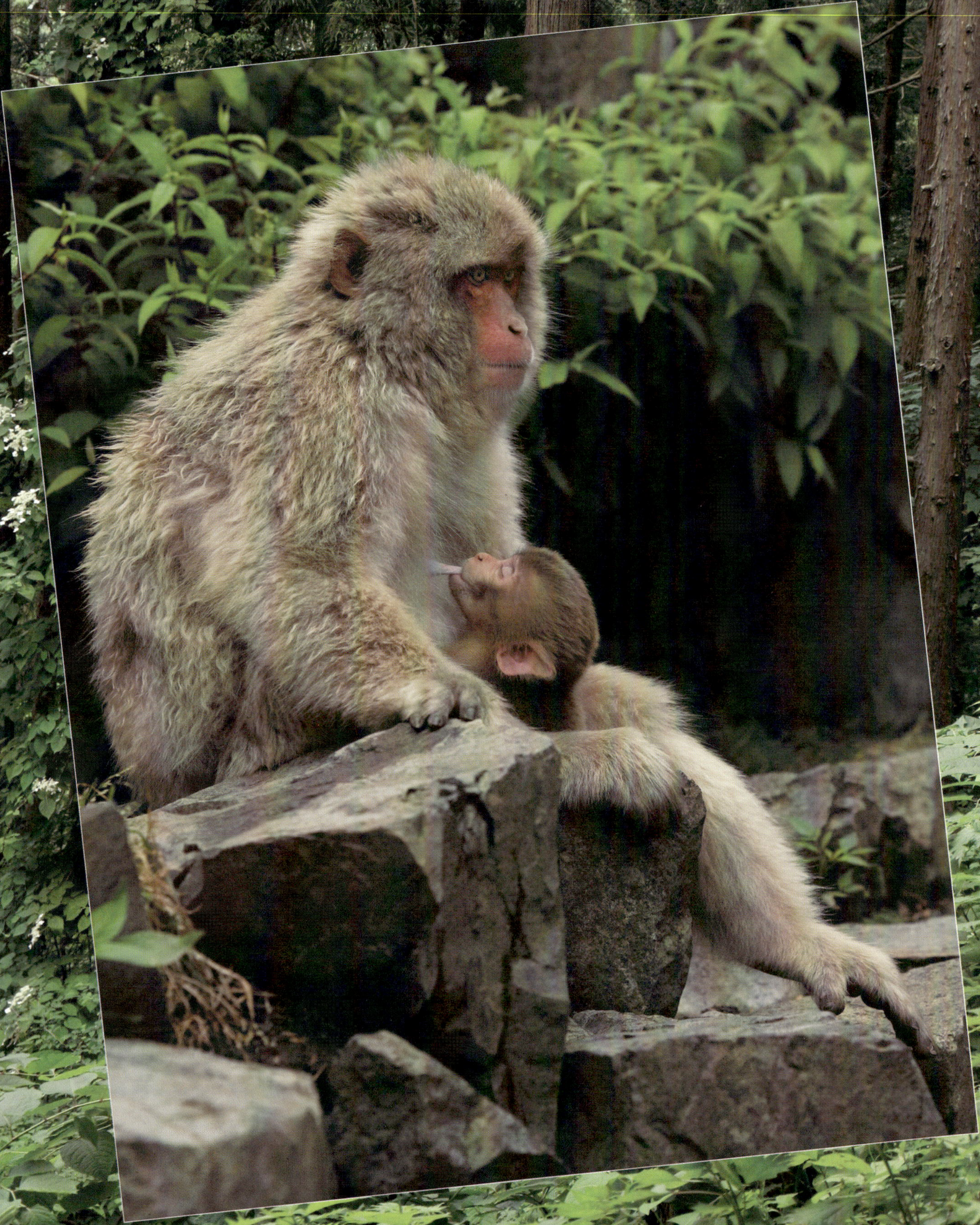

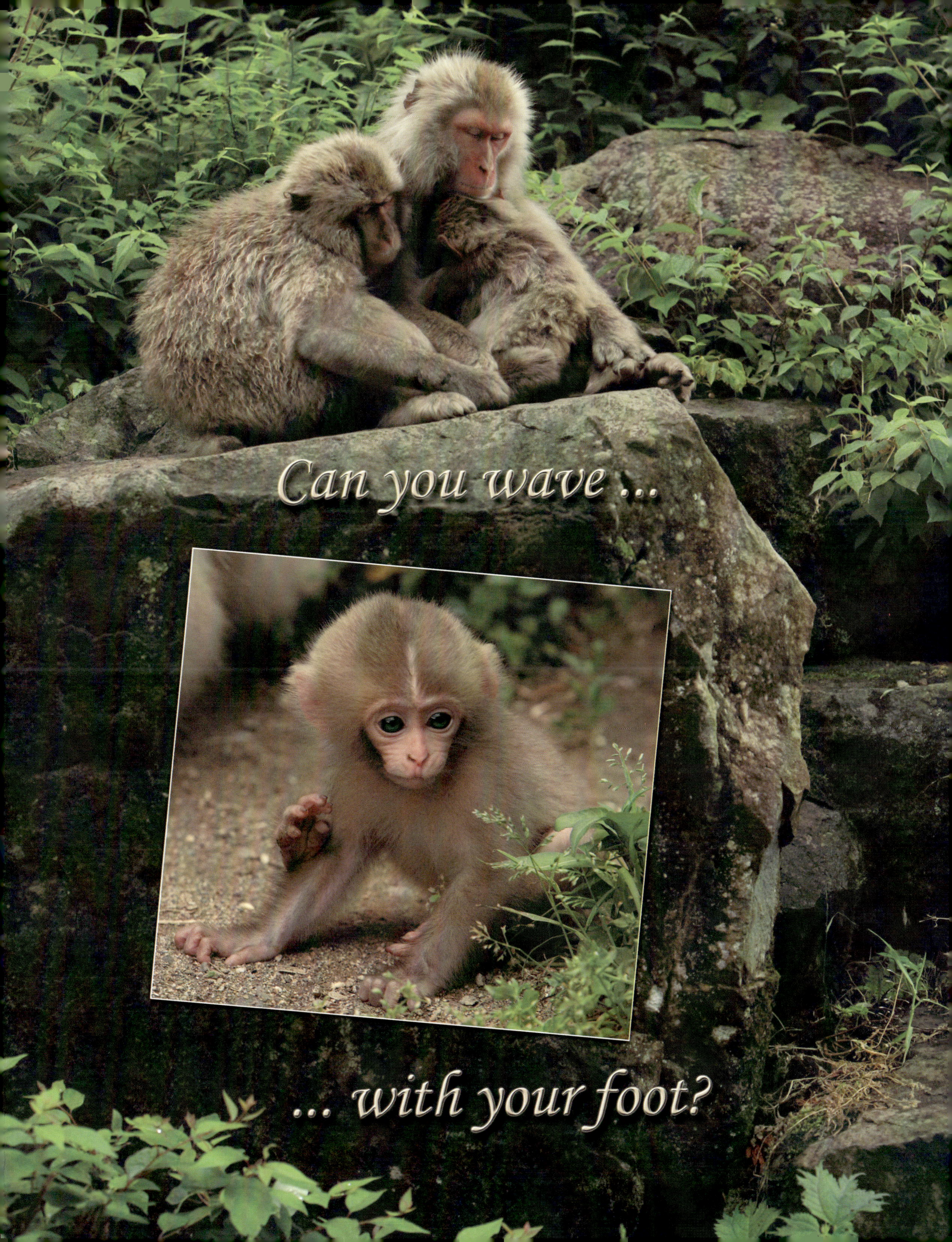

Can you wave ...

... with your foot?

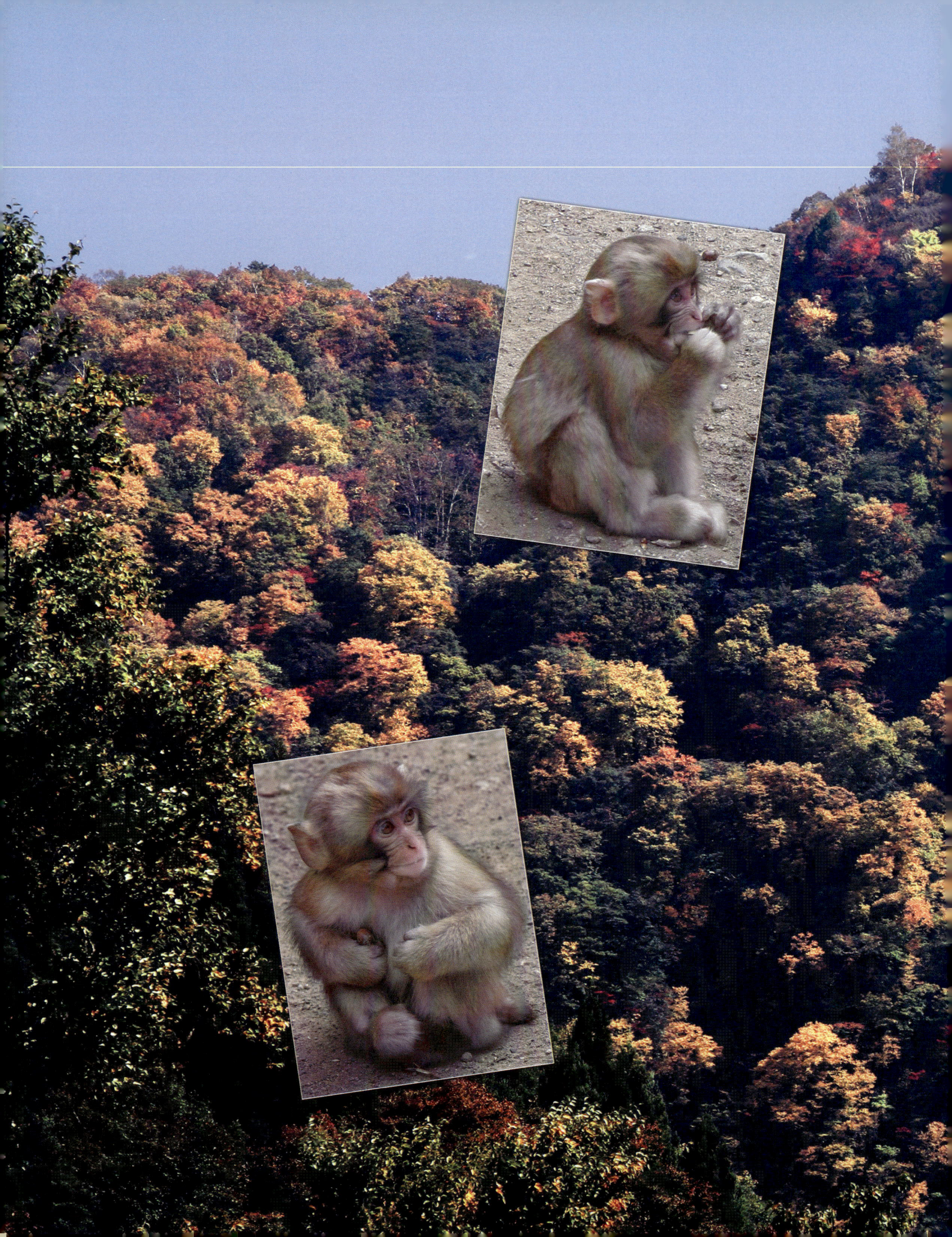

At times like this, I wish that I had a nut-cracker (a kitchen tool to open hard nuts).

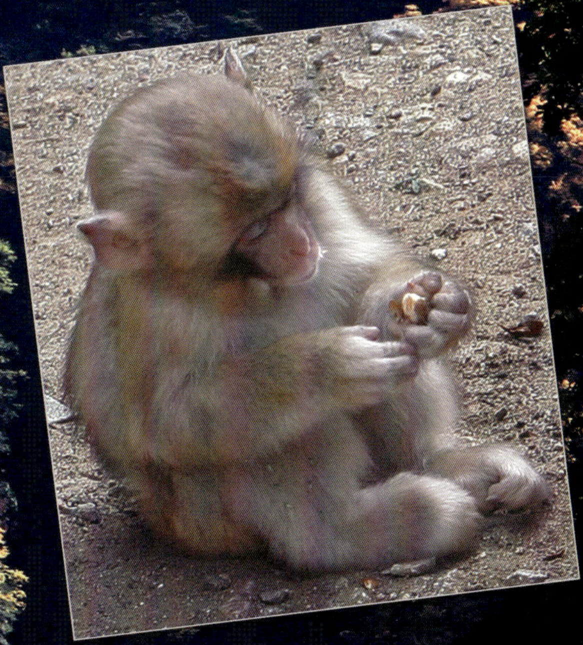

My Dad is taking a short nap.

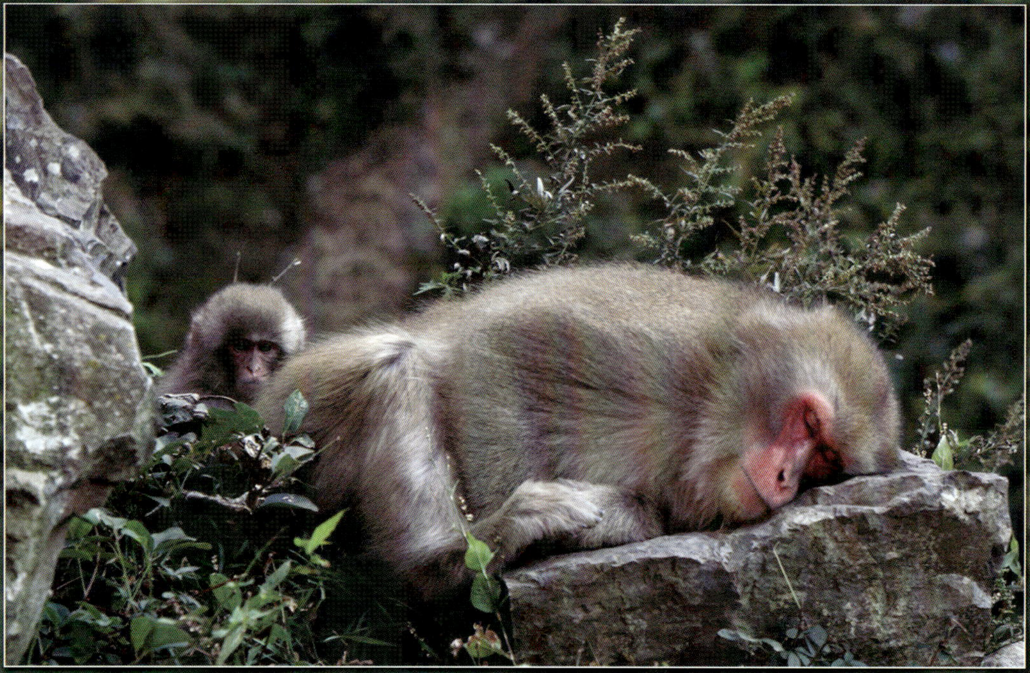

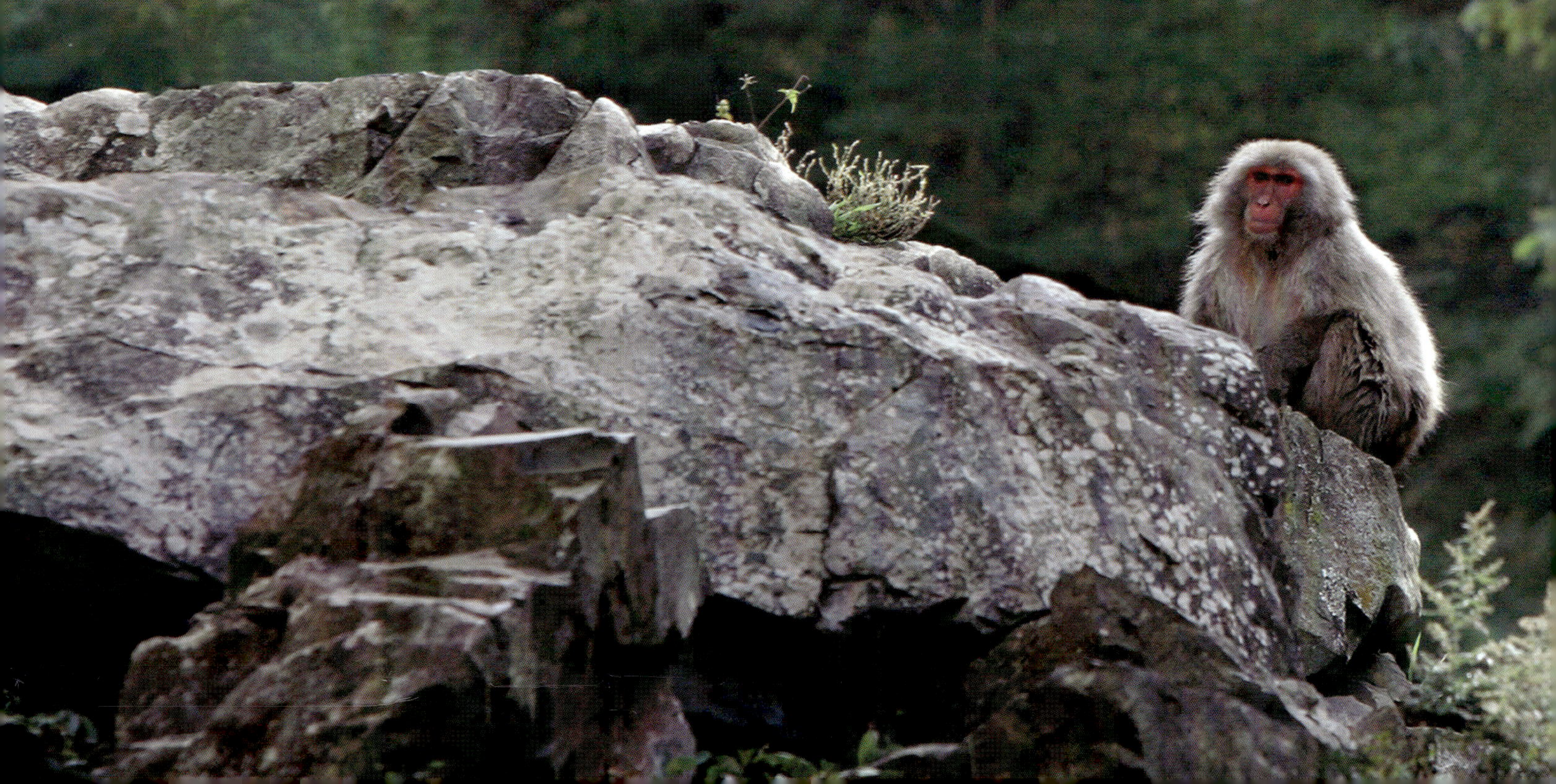

Some monkeys think that my dad has a big mouth.

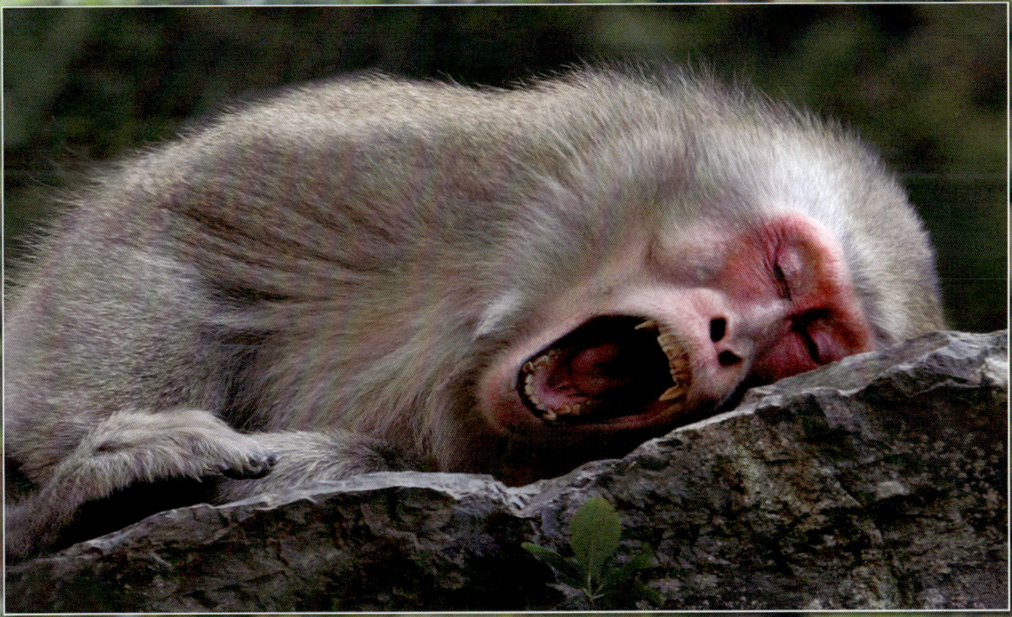

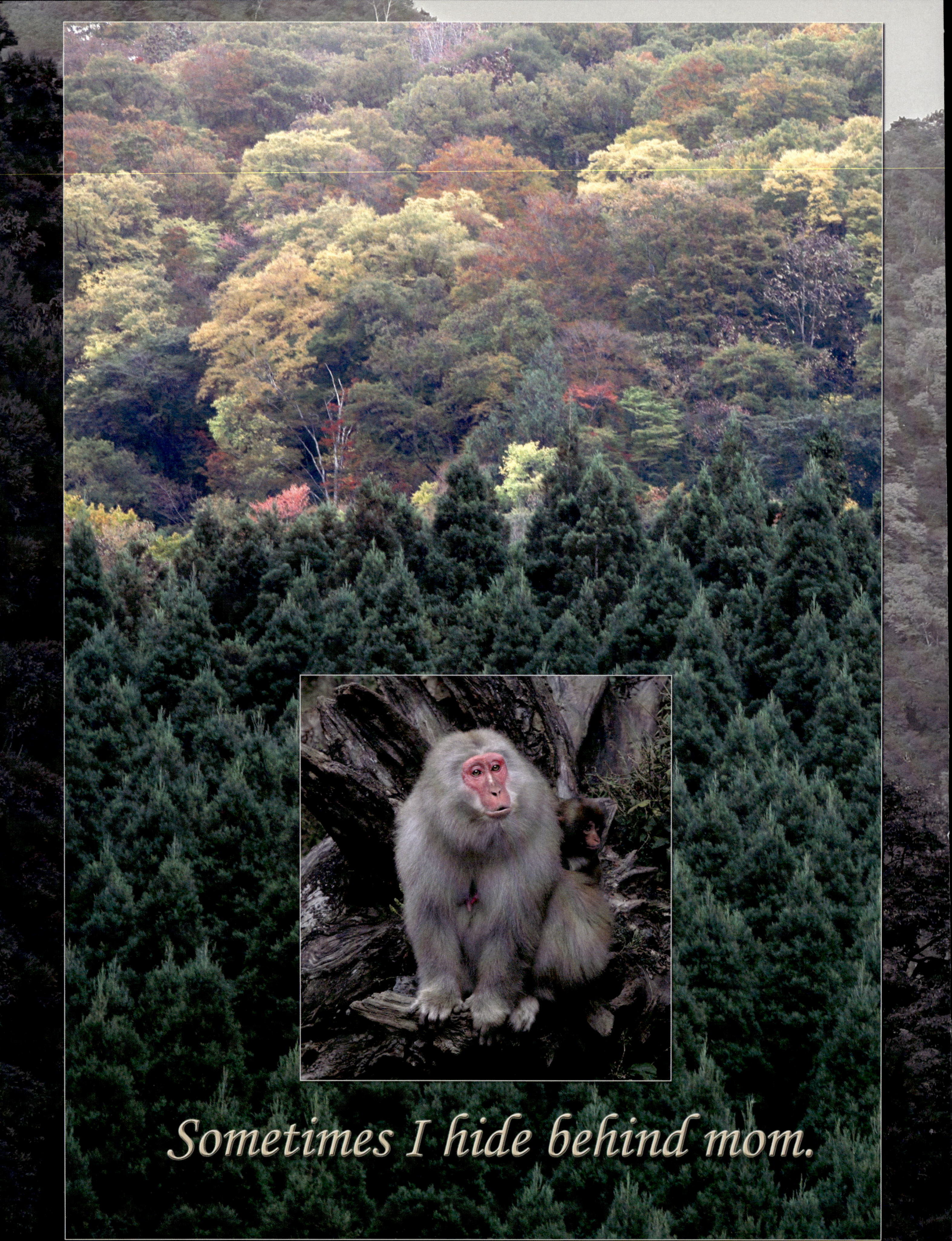

Sometimes I hide behind mom.

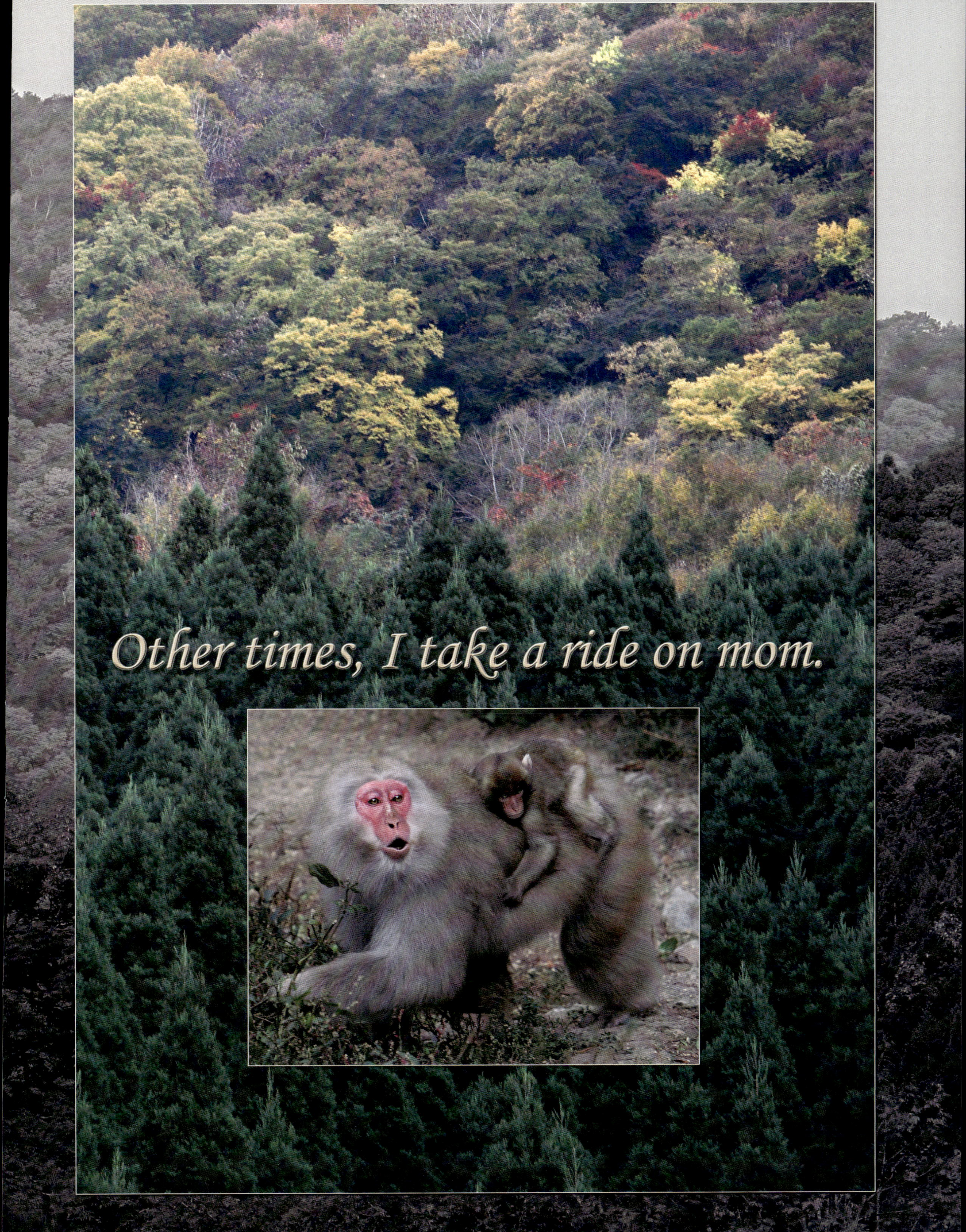

Other times, I take a ride on mom.

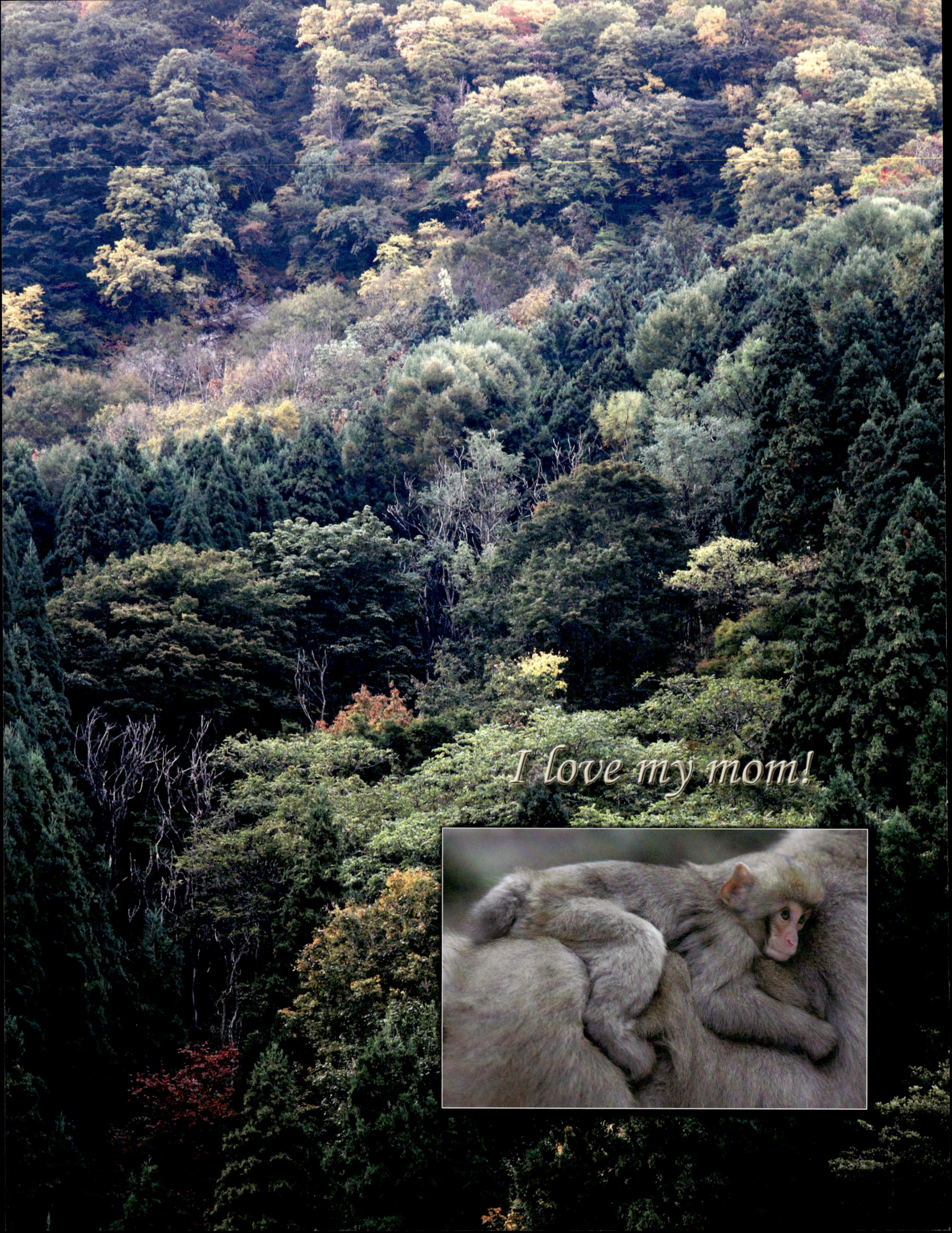

I love my mom!

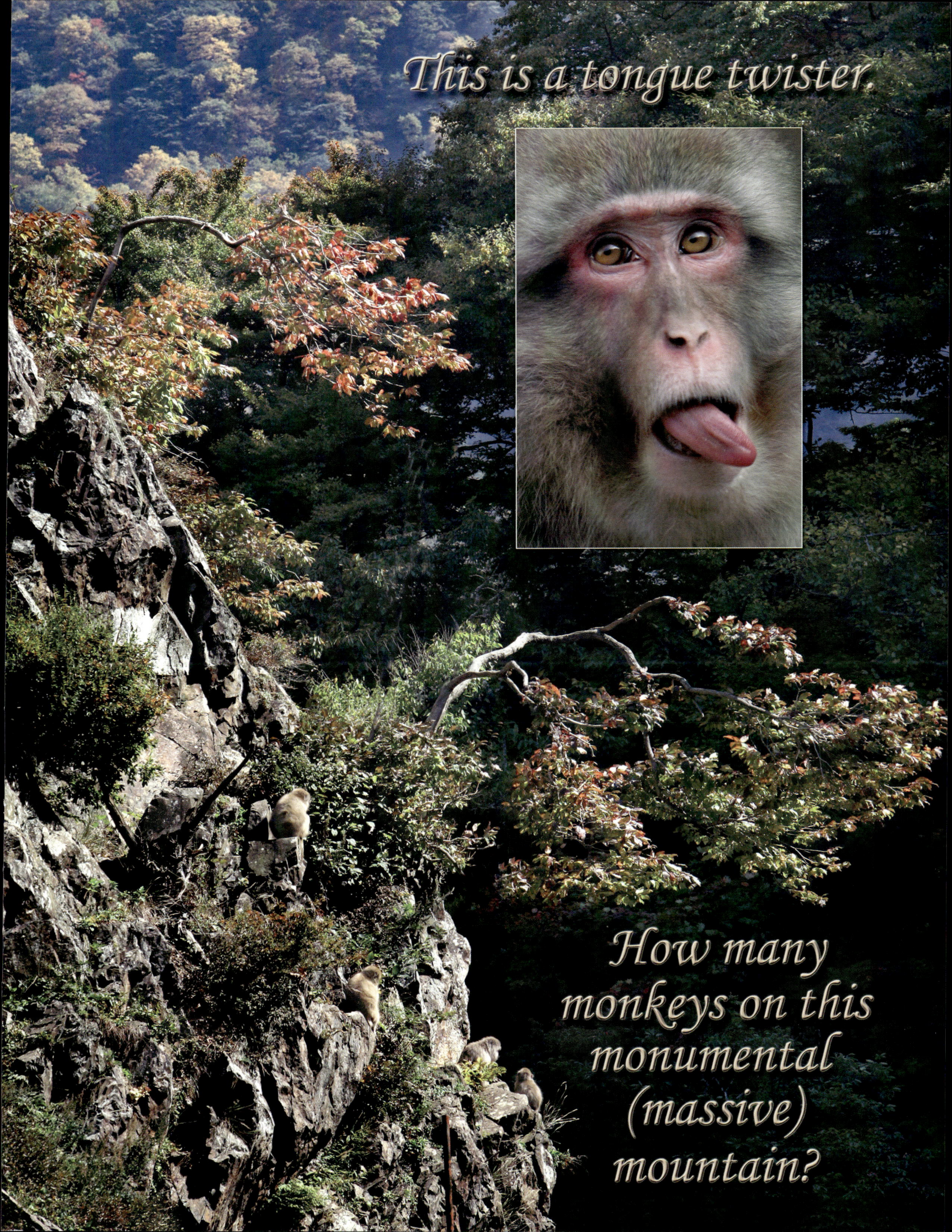

This is a tongue twister.

How many monkeys on this monumental (massive) mountain?

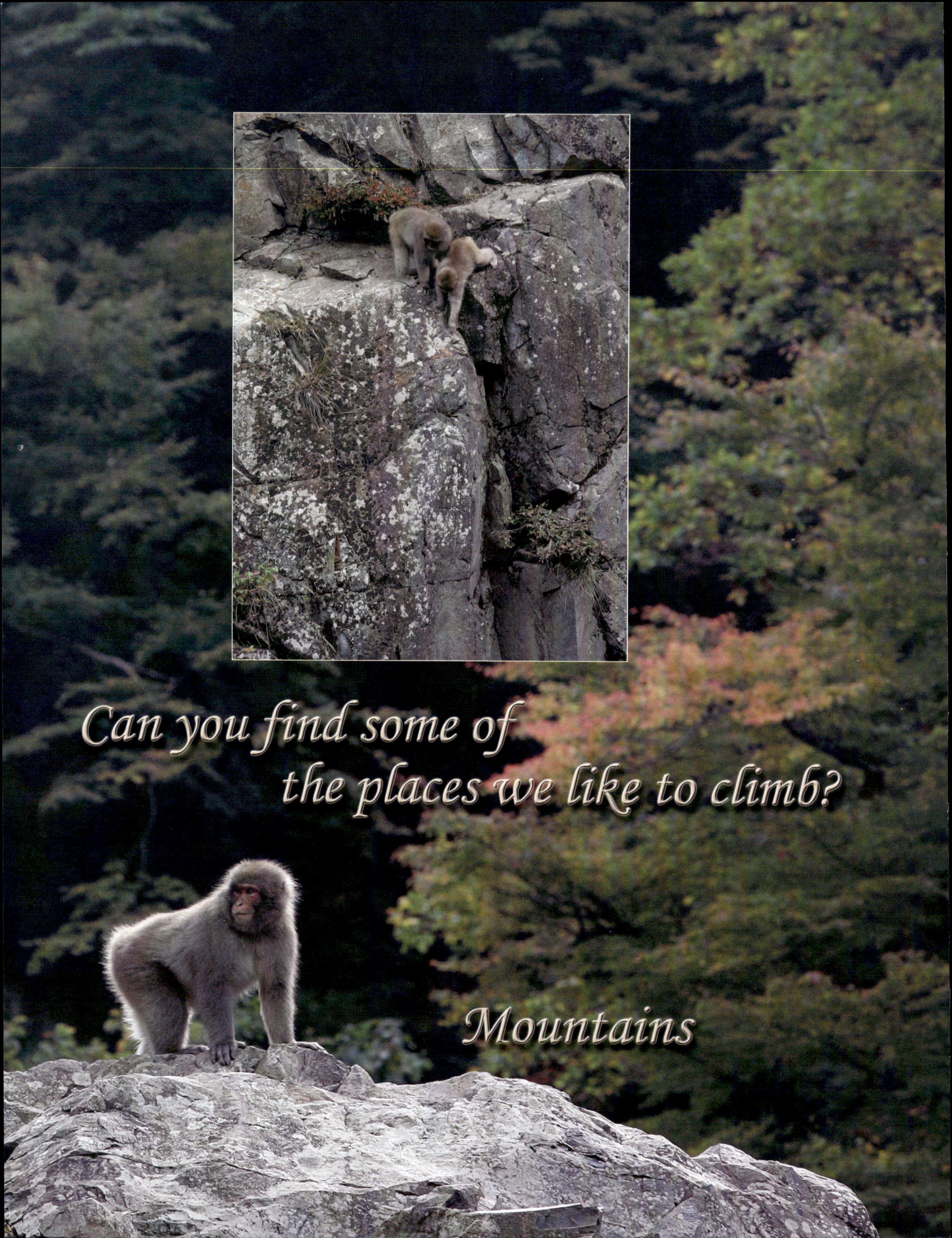

Can you find some of the places we like to climb?

Mountains

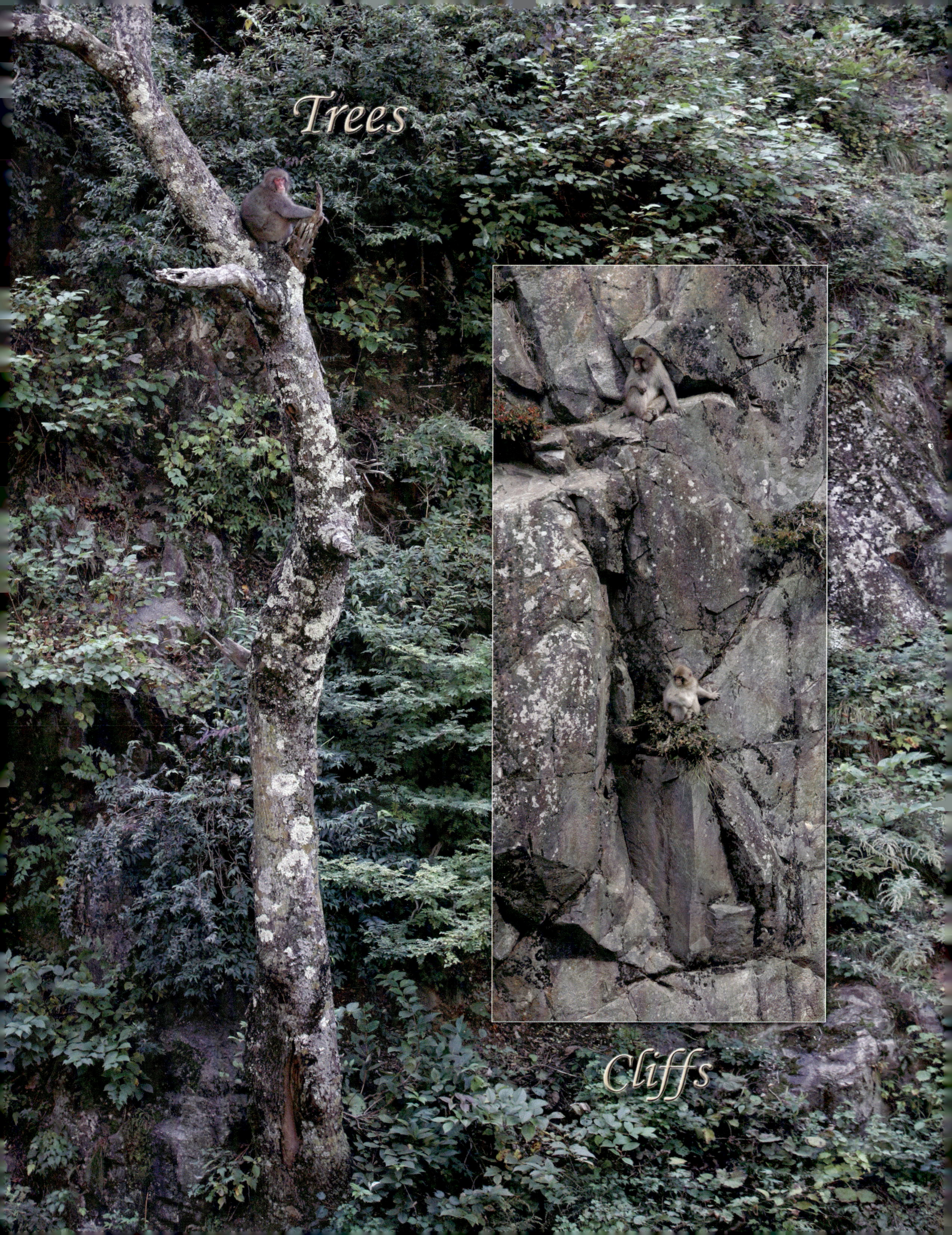
Trees
Cliffs

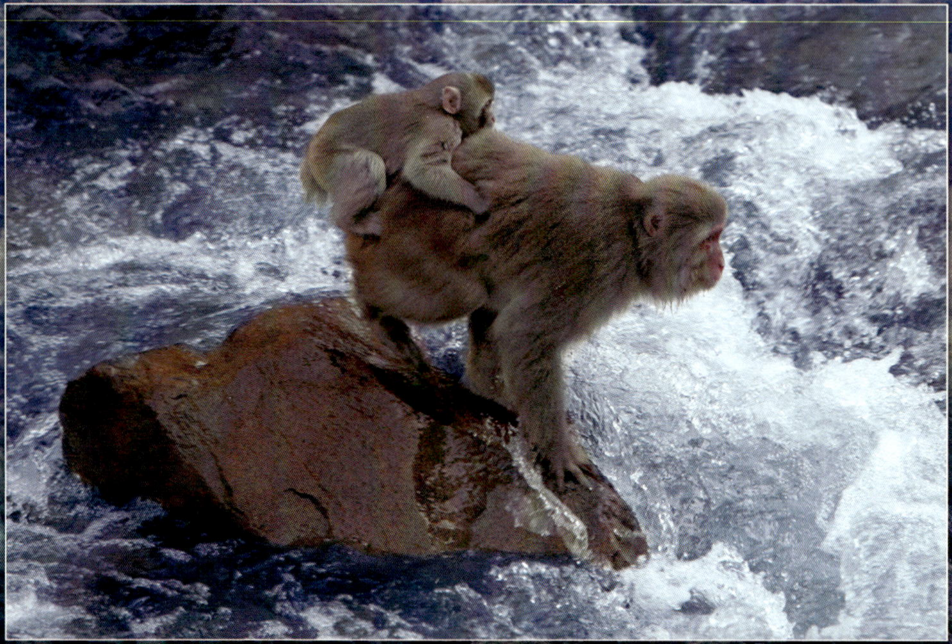

For times like these ...

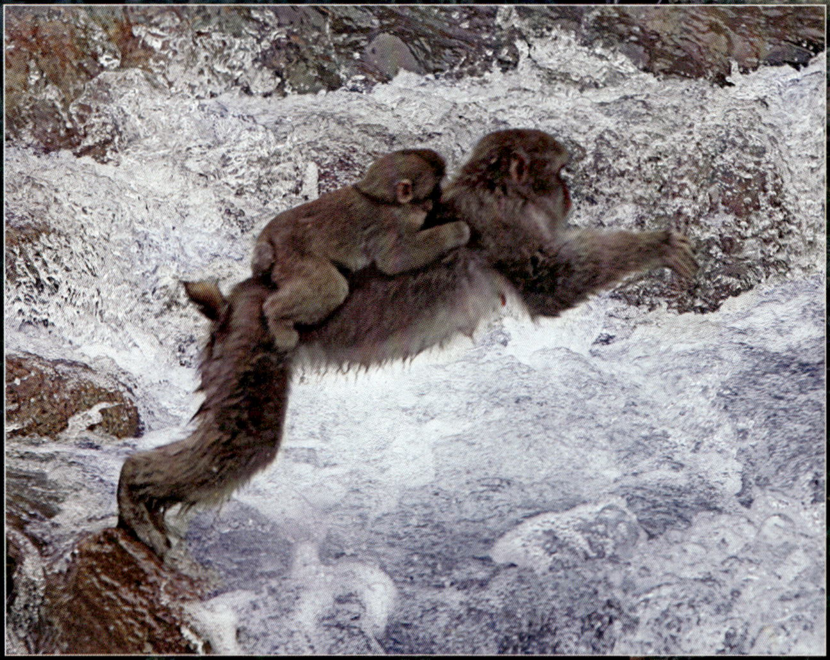

...I wish I had a seat belt.

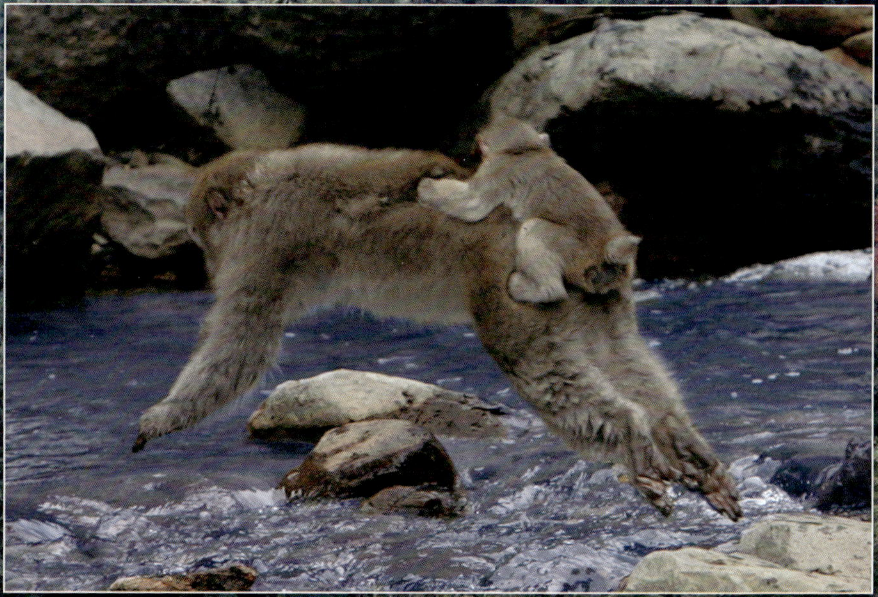

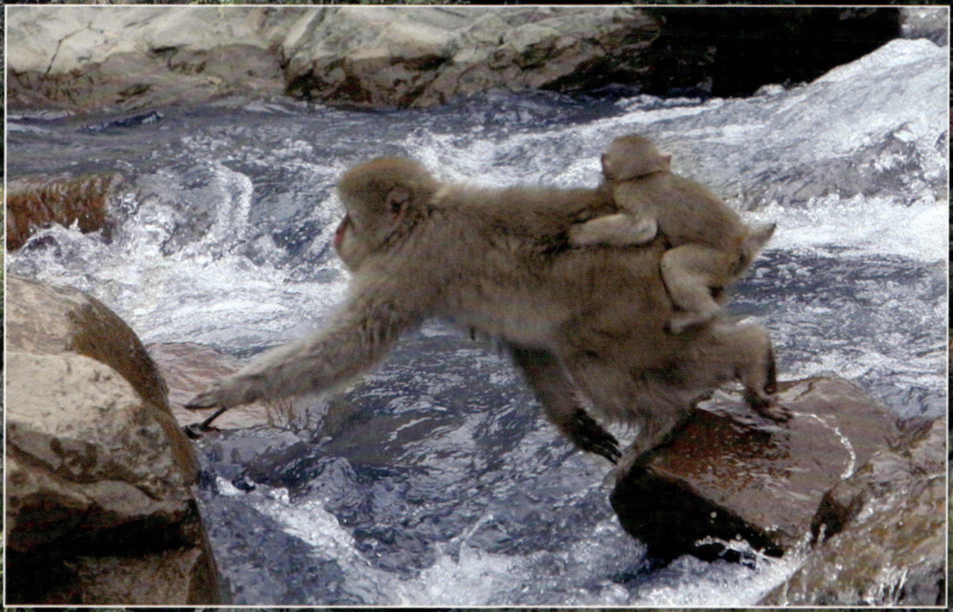

Do you wear seat belts?

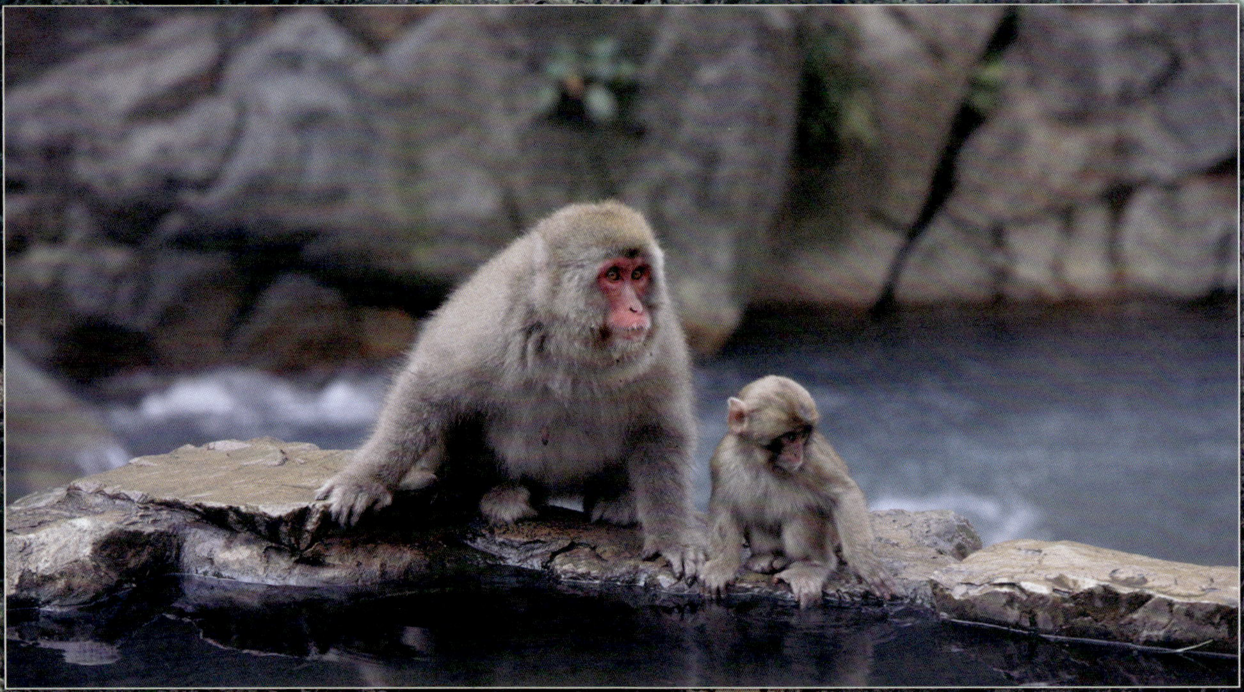

My dad is twice as tall as I am.

Now I am higher than he is.

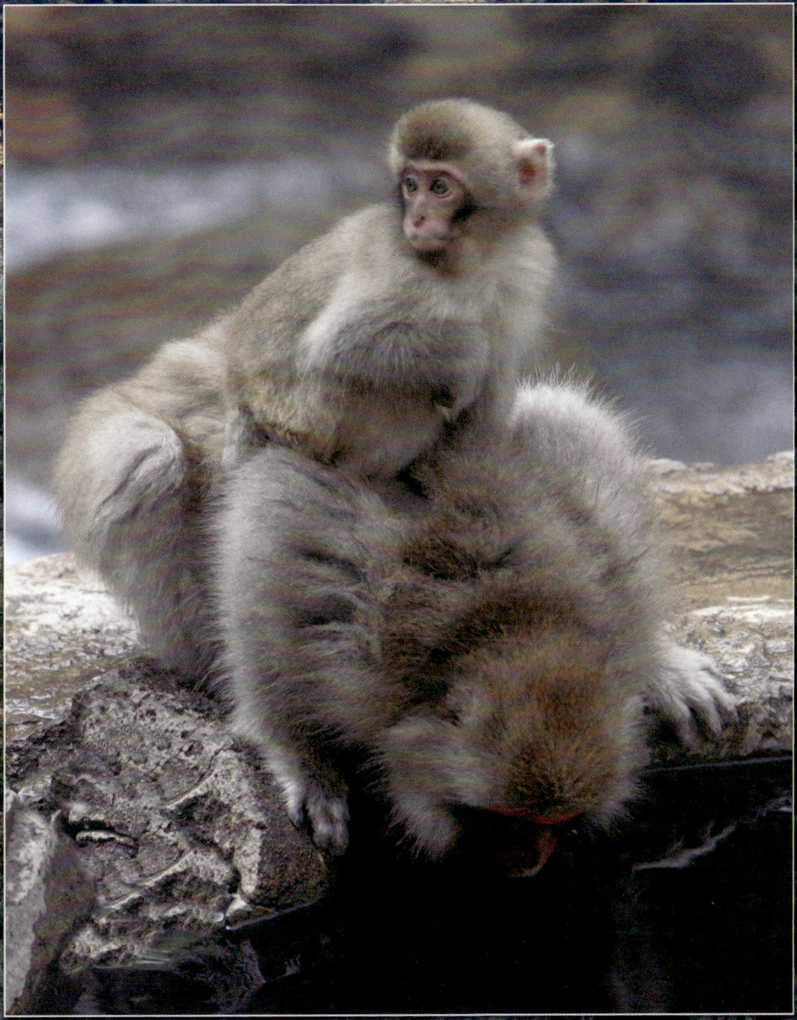

Are you taller than your dad?

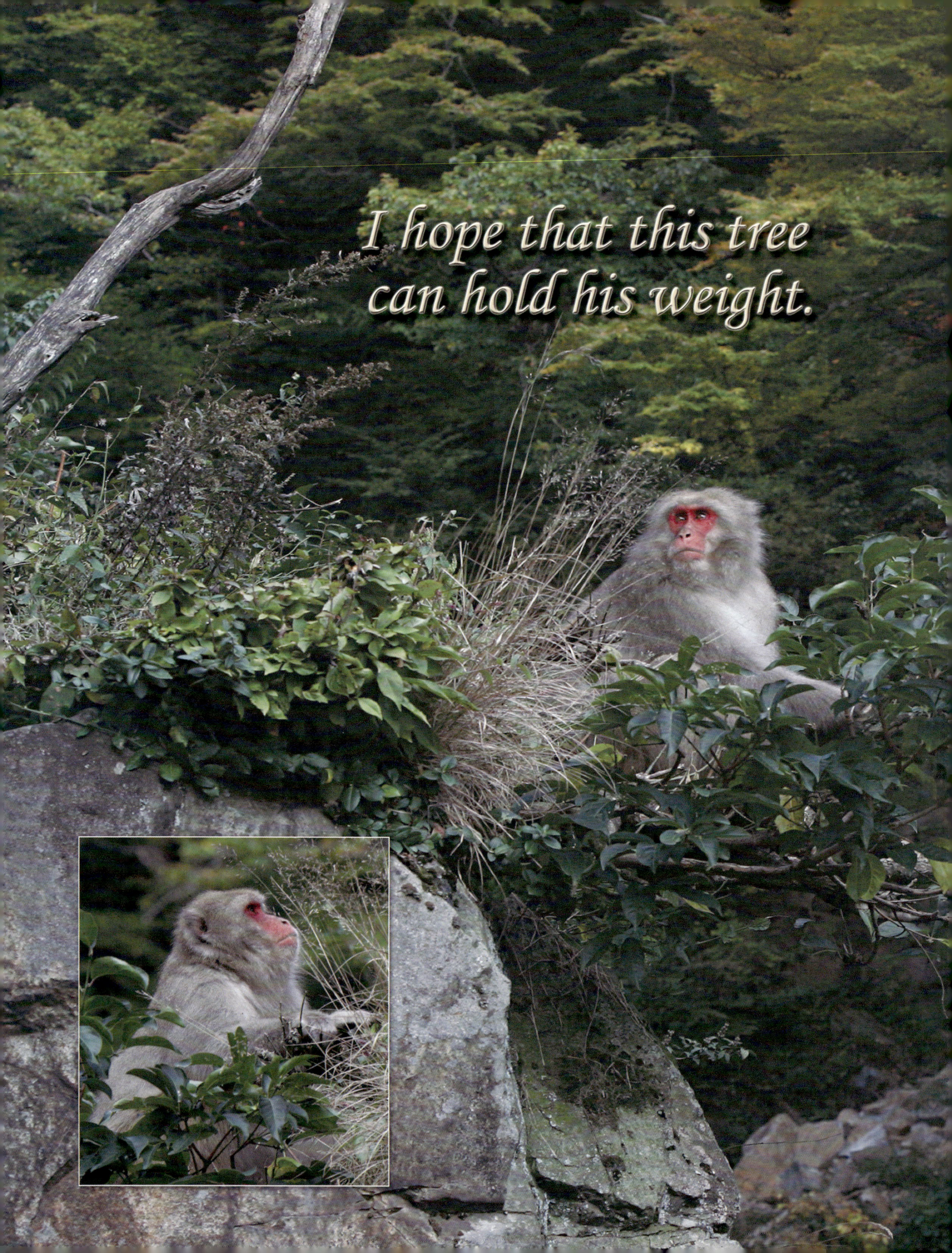

I hope that this tree can hold his weight.

This snow monkey weighs 66 lbs.

Do you weigh more or less than this monkey?

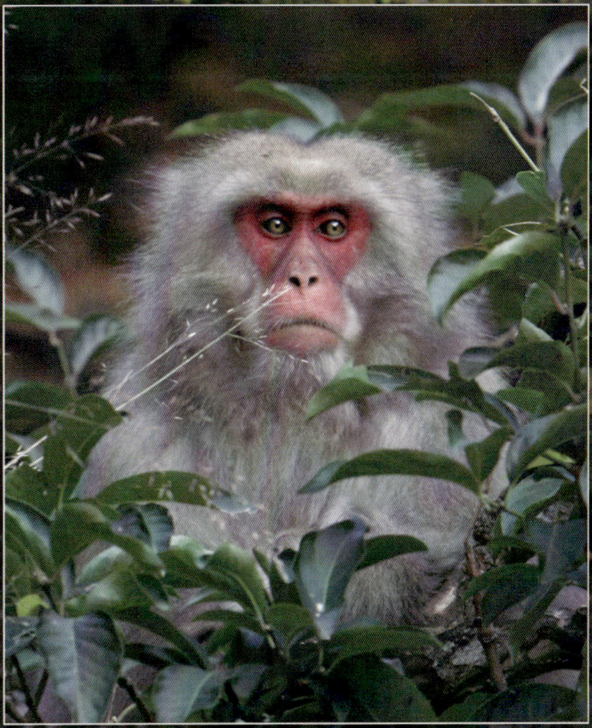

In fall, the head monkey

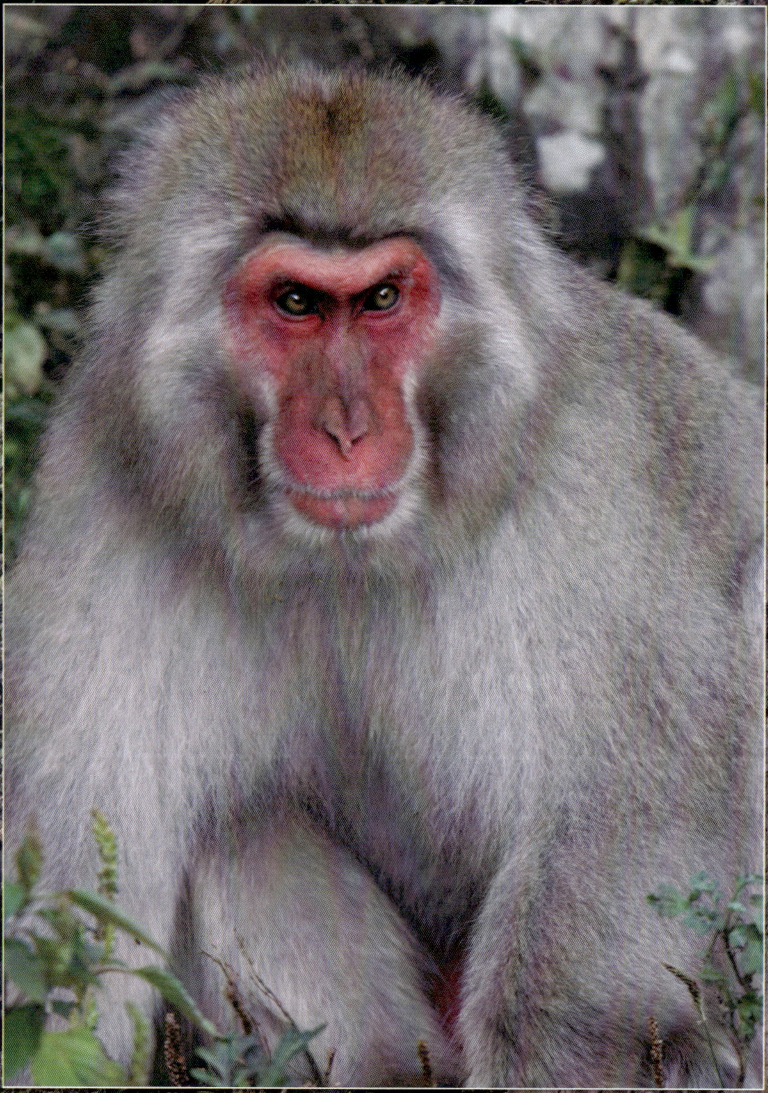

gets mean, and we all ...

... climb away

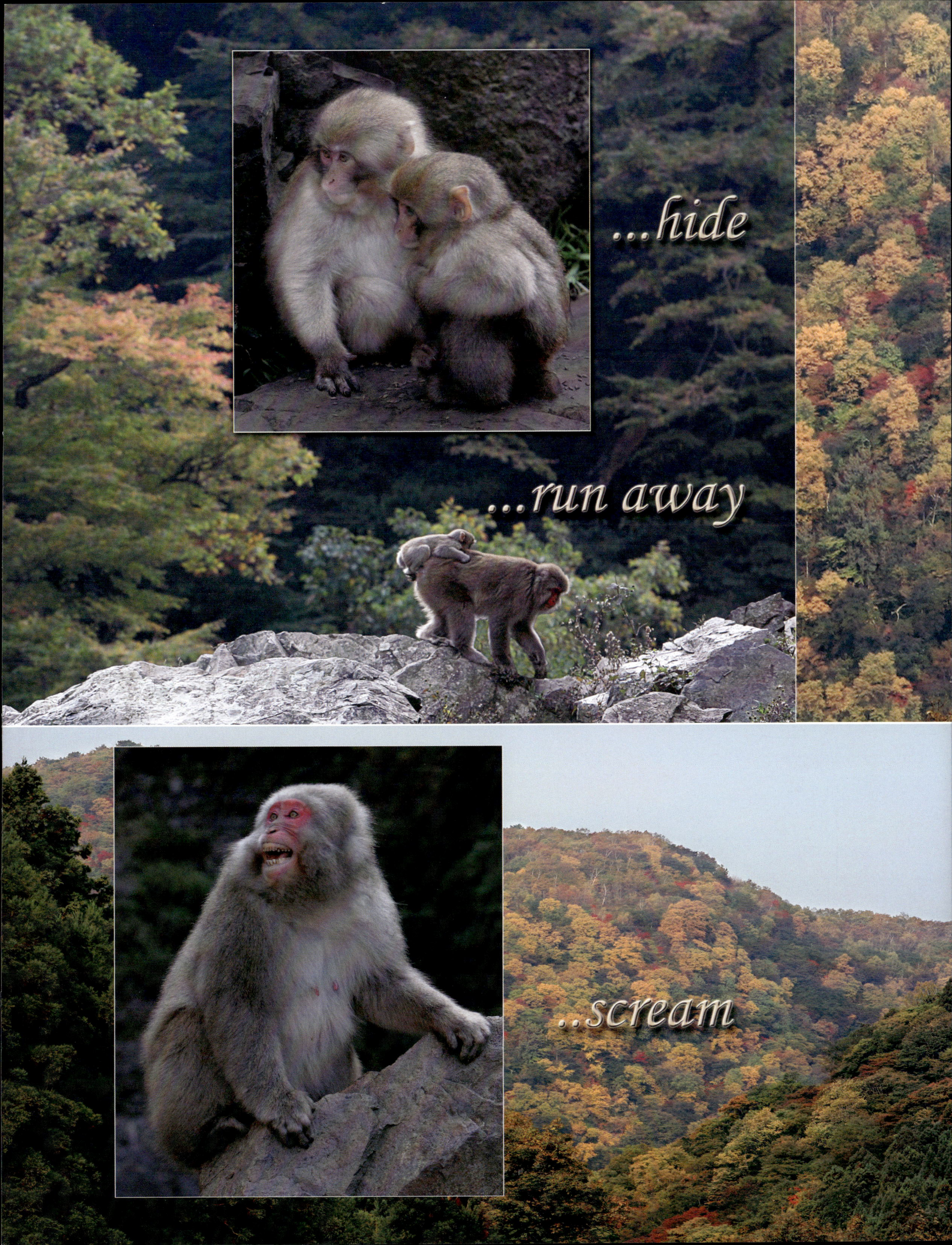
...hide
...run away
..scream

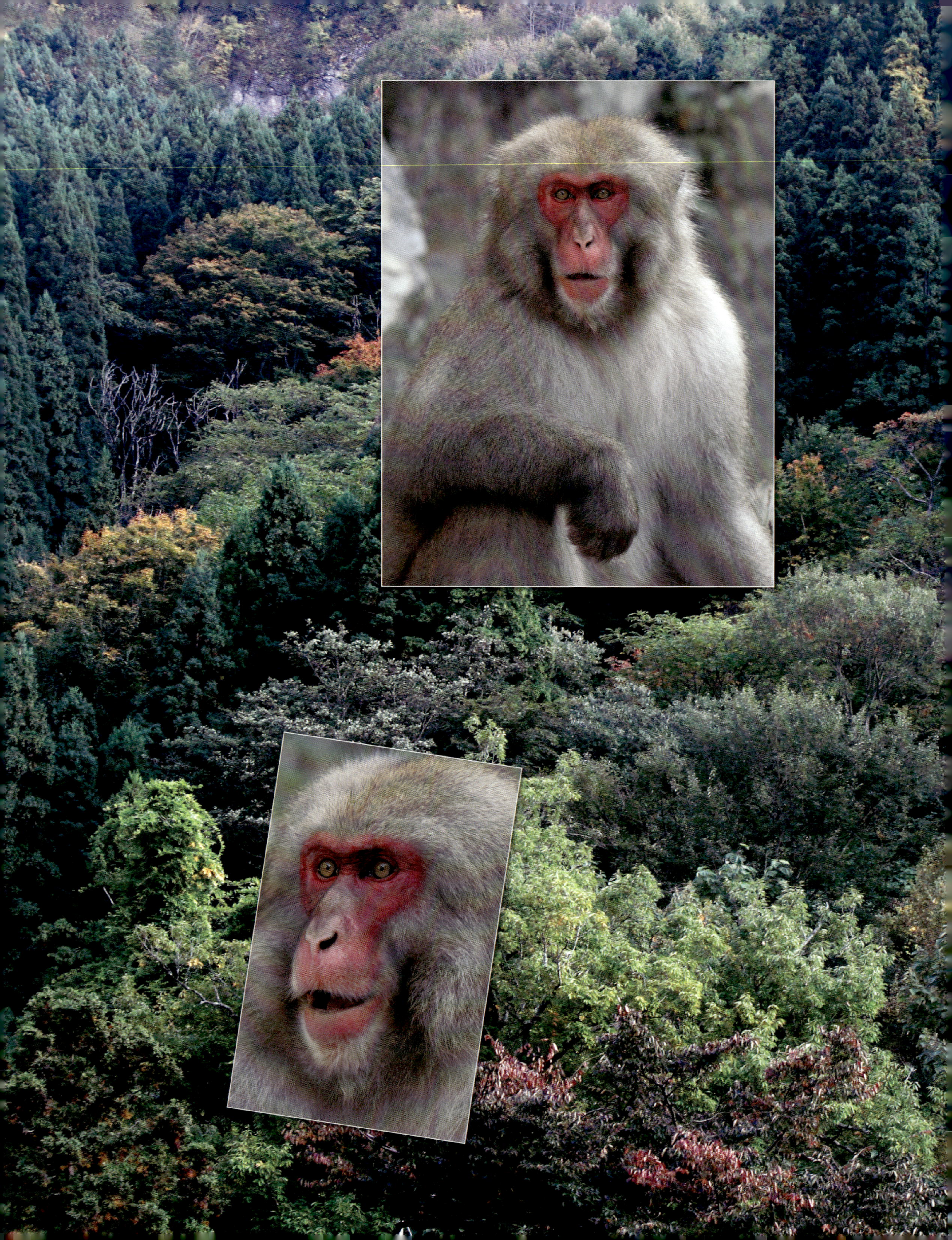

Can you find where this adult snow monkey is ...

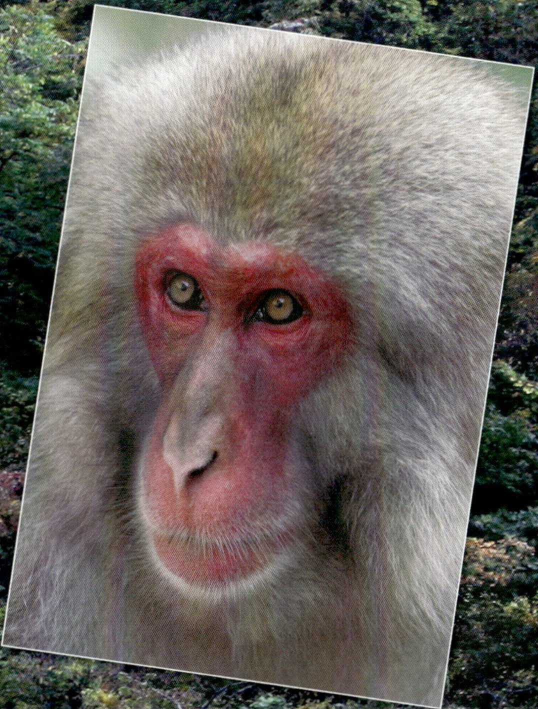

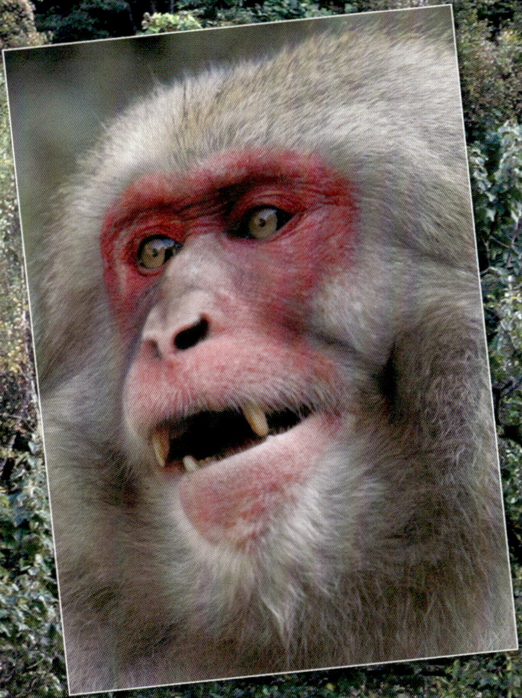

1) Serious

2) Laughing

3) Relaxing

4) Smiling

Everyone should make
a yearly trip to see ...

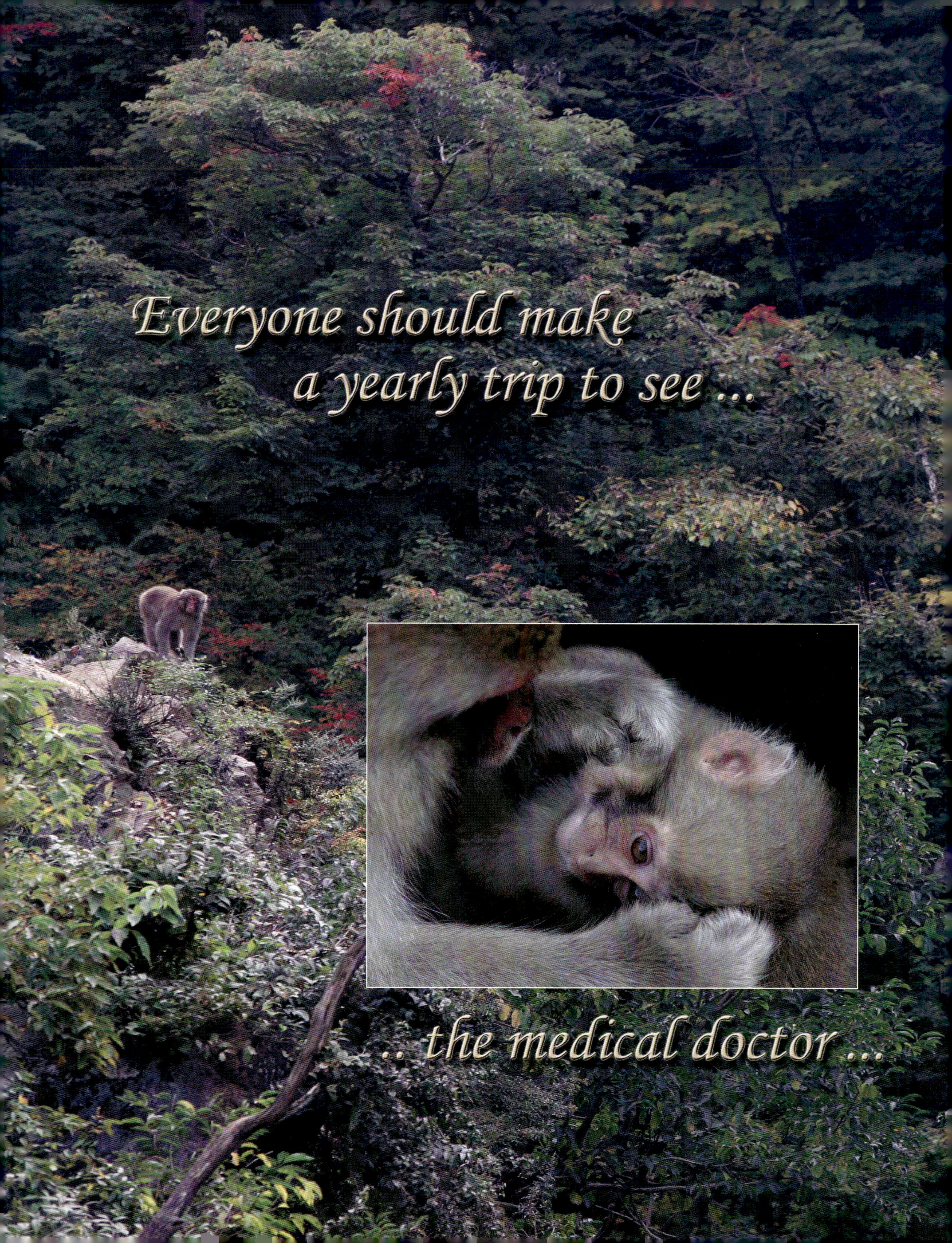

.. the medical doctor ...

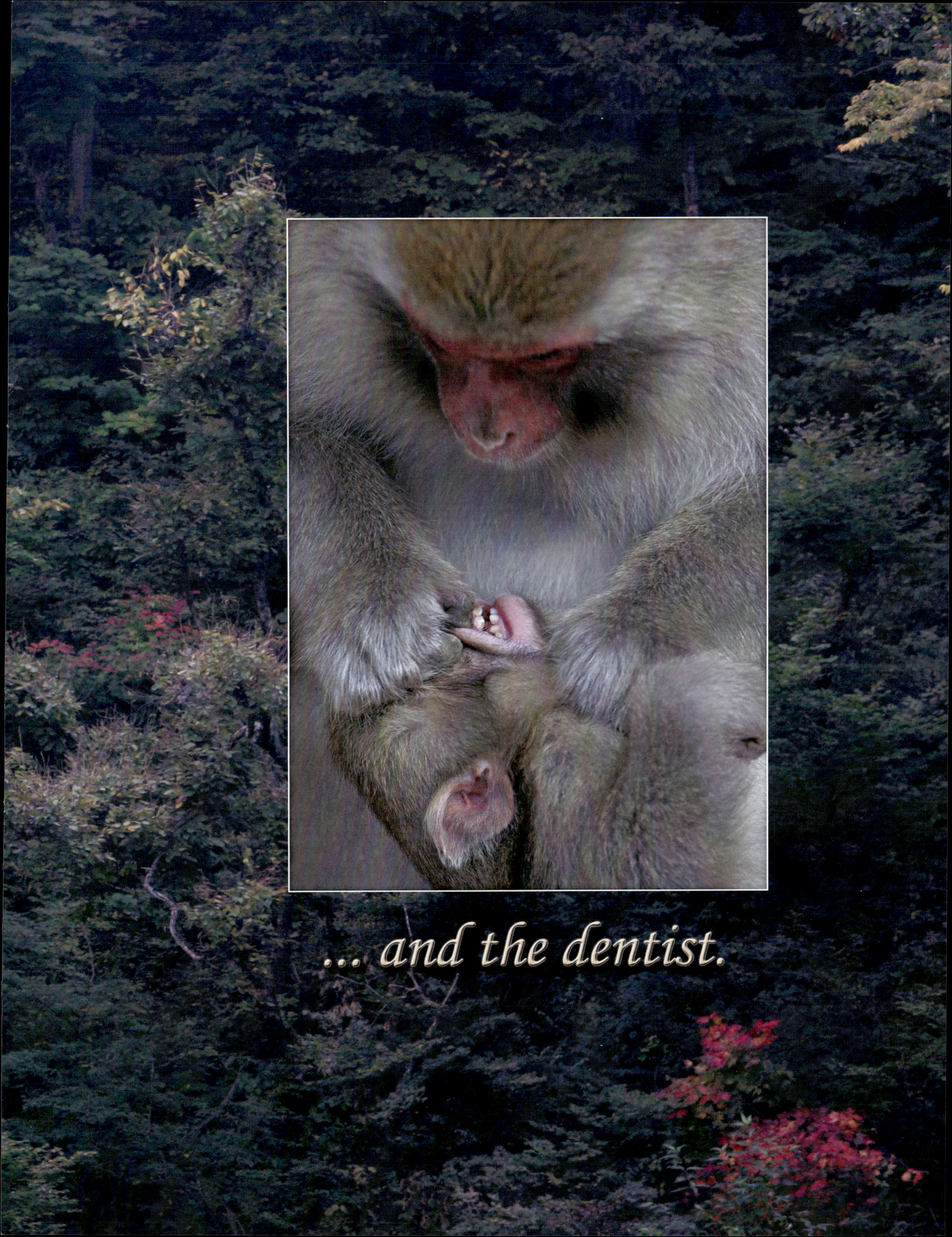

… and the dentist.

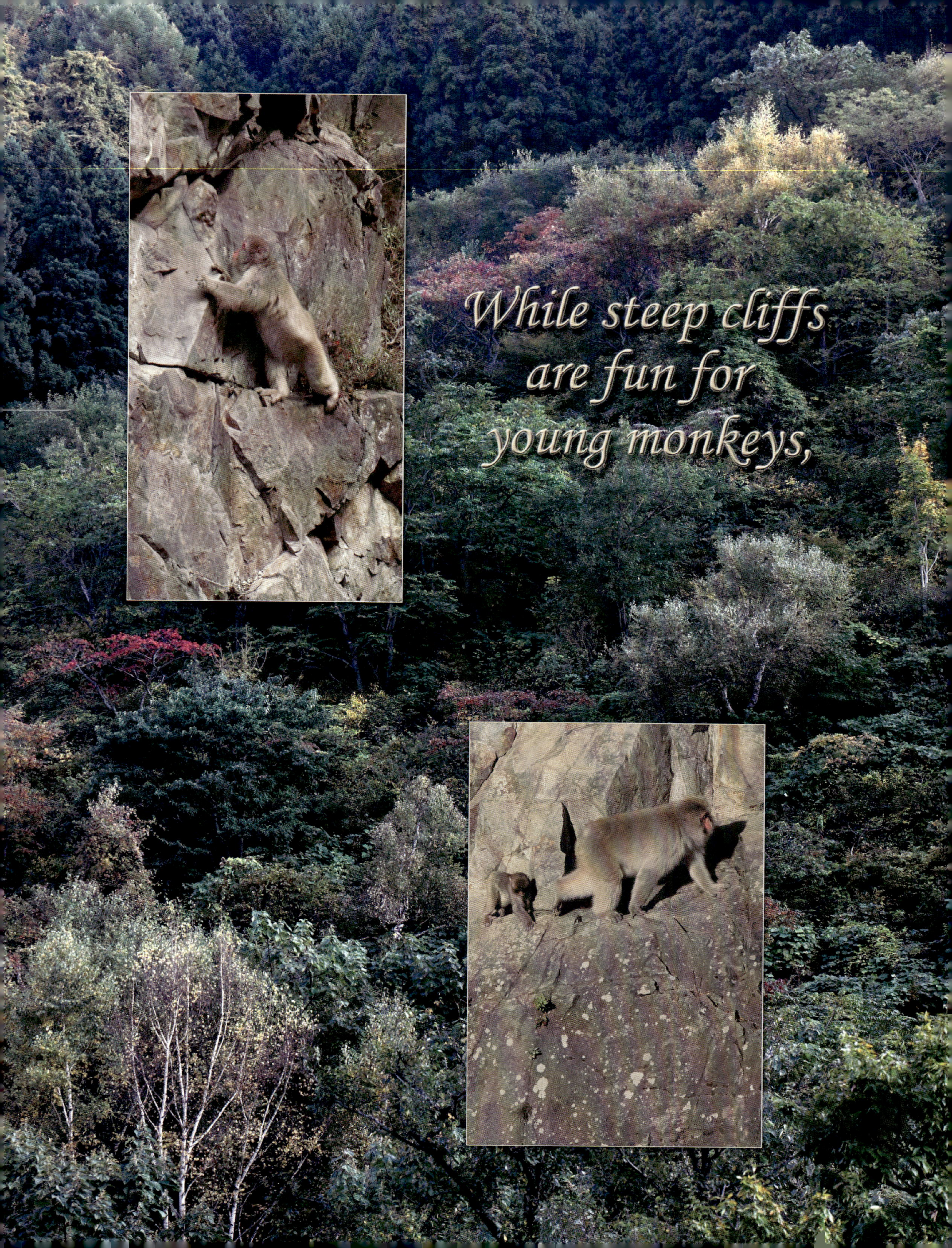

While steep cliffs are fun for young monkeys,

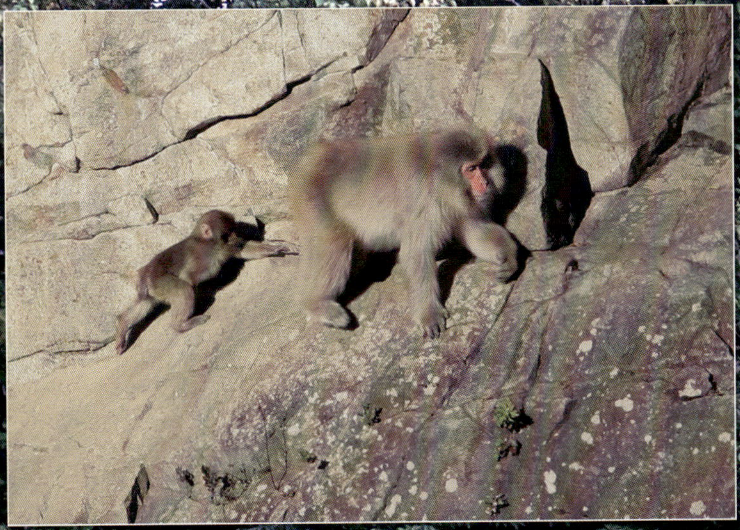

You should only try this if you are Spider-Man, Batman, or Superman.

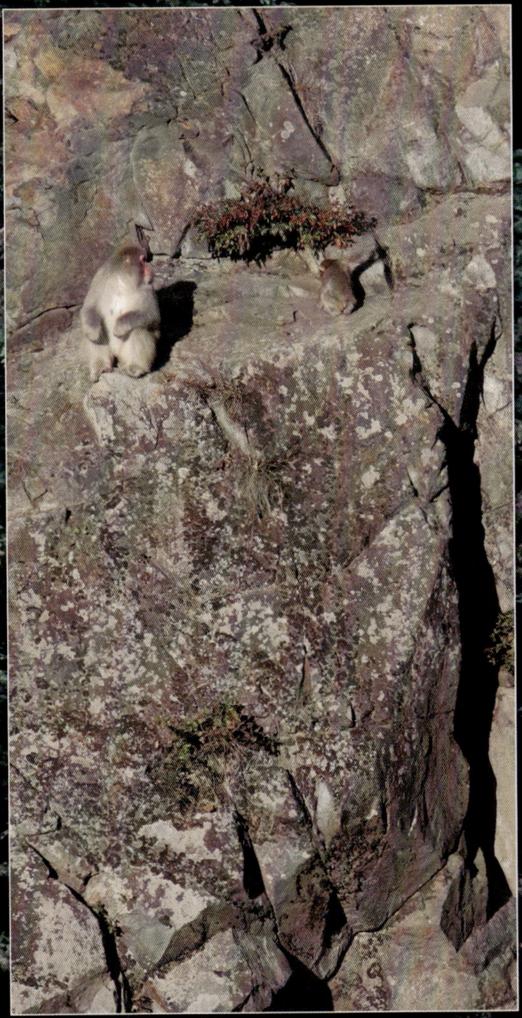

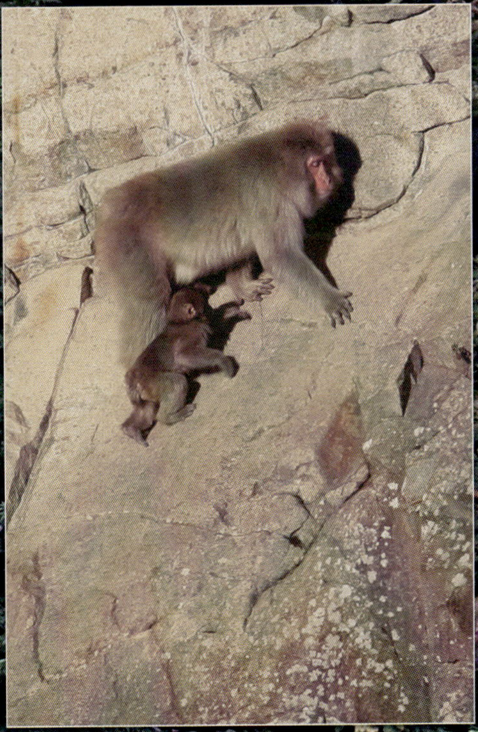

Each day has its "ups"...

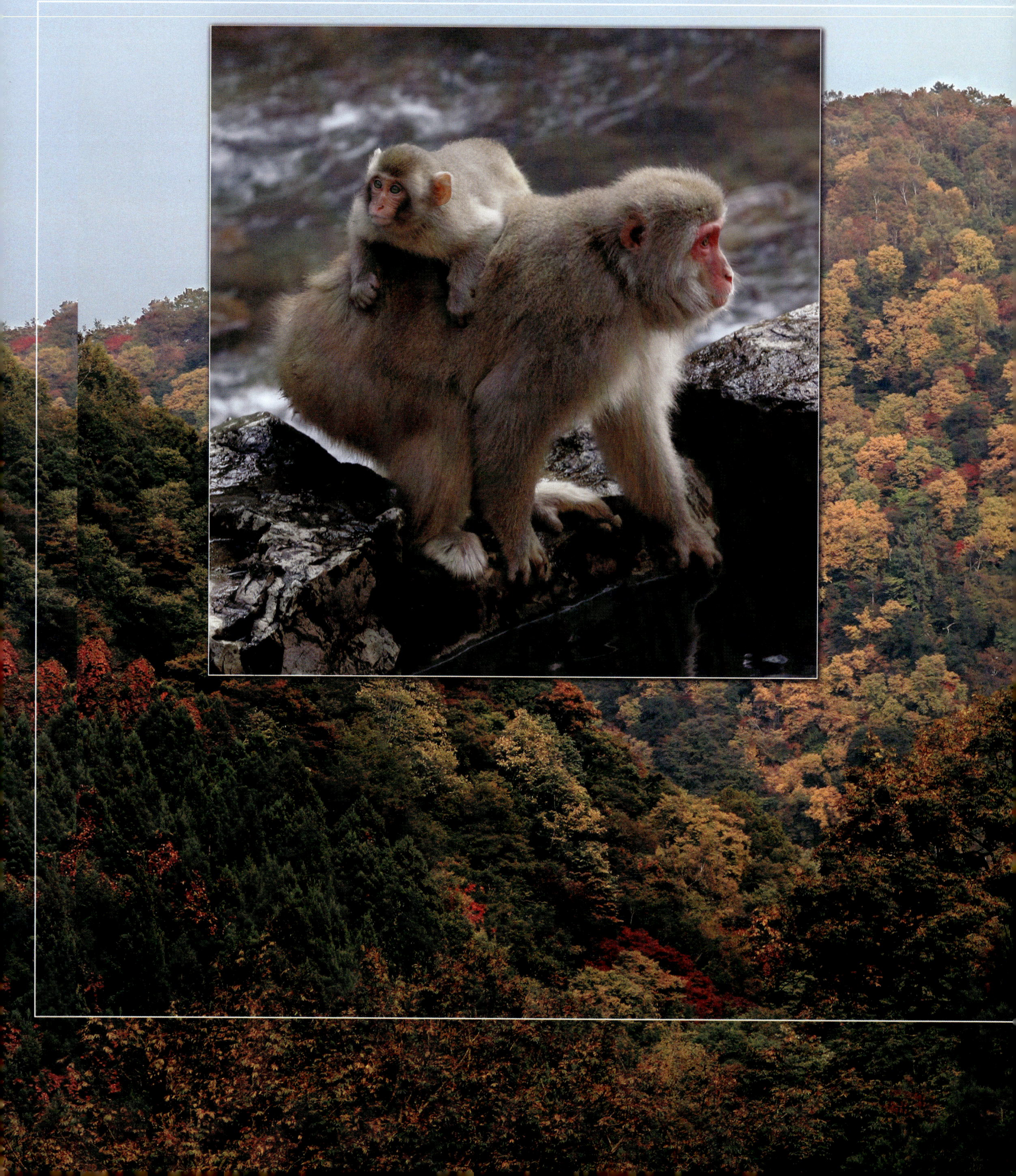

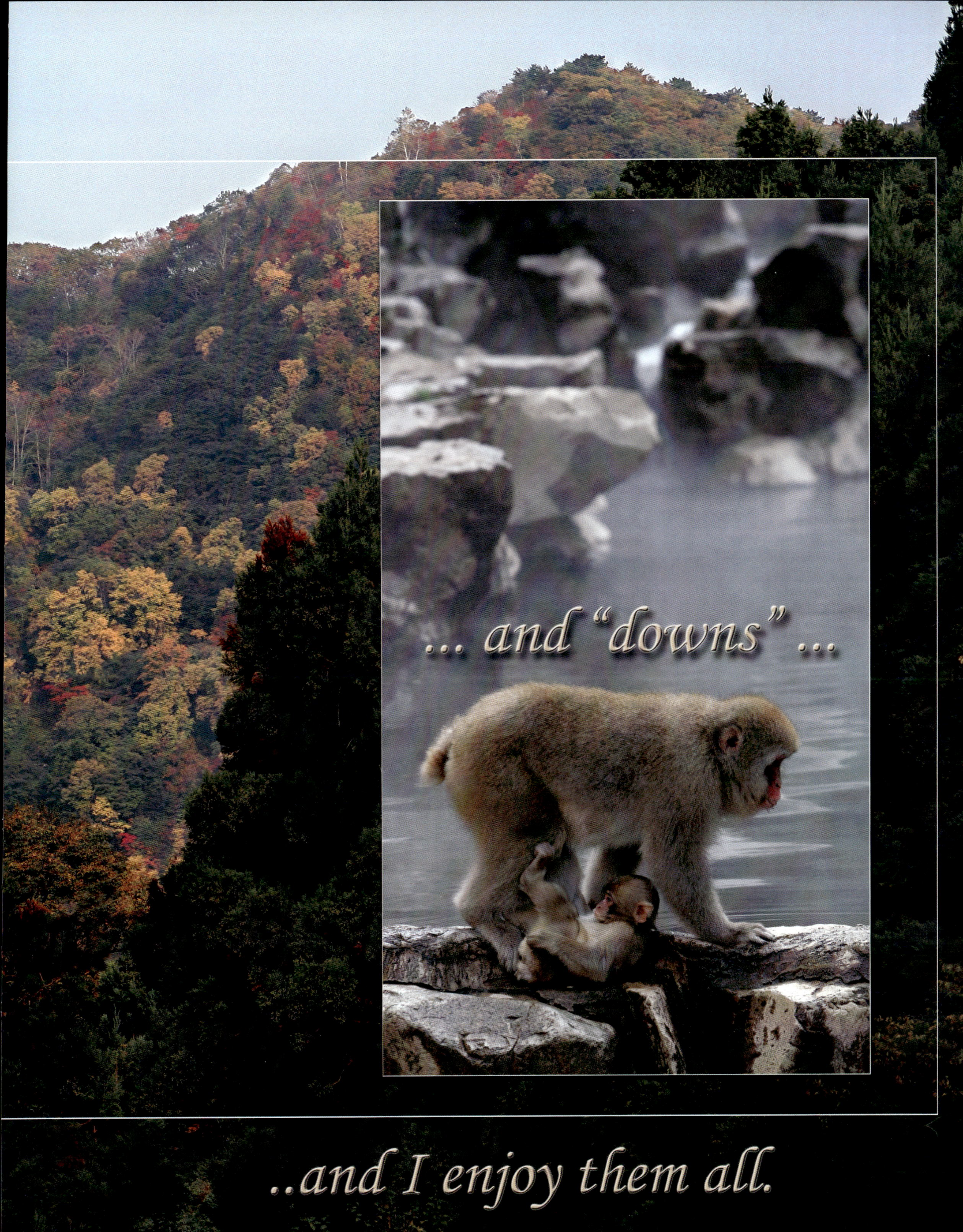
... and "downs" ...
..and I enjoy them all.

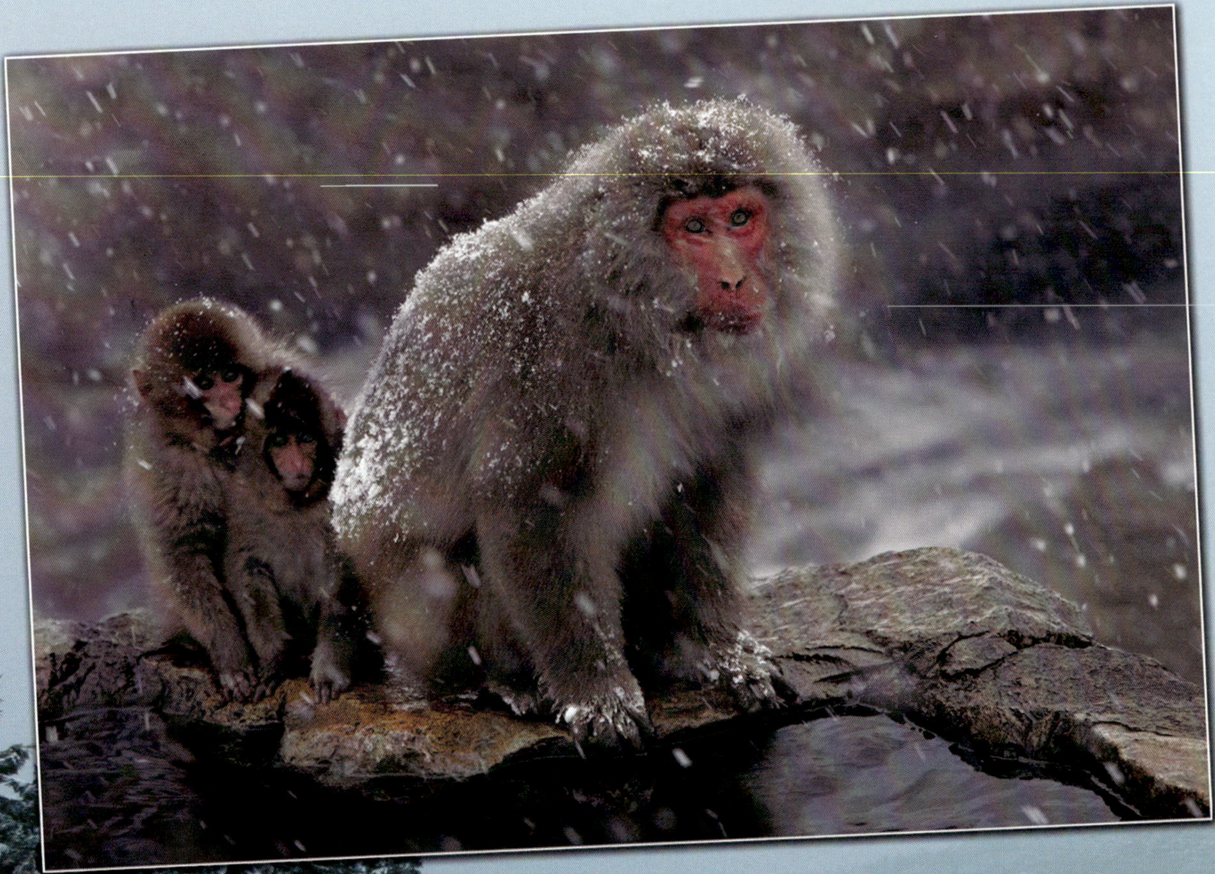

In the winter, we grow a heavy insulating coat to maintain our body temperature.

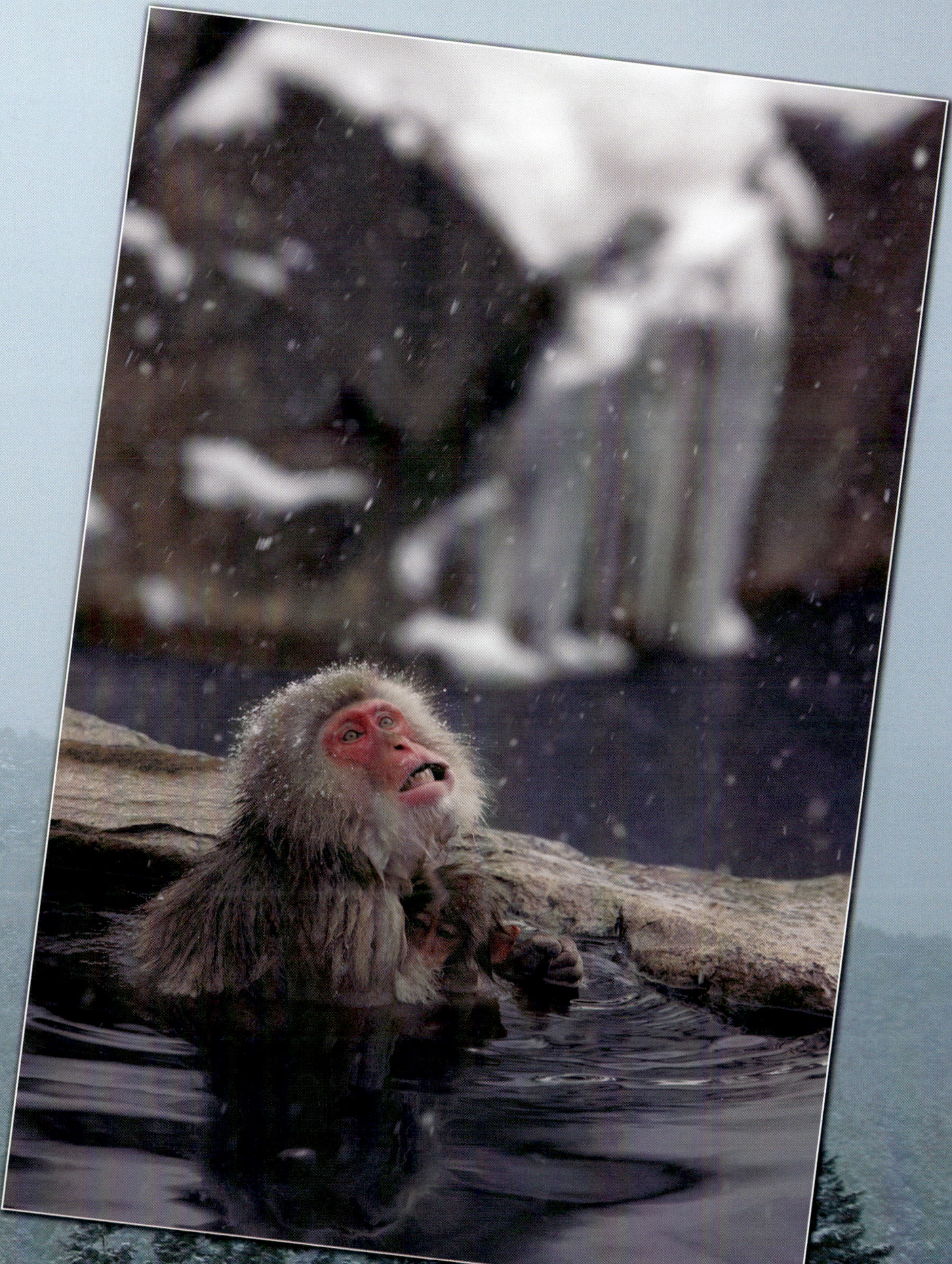

Winter has arrived with cold weather and snow.

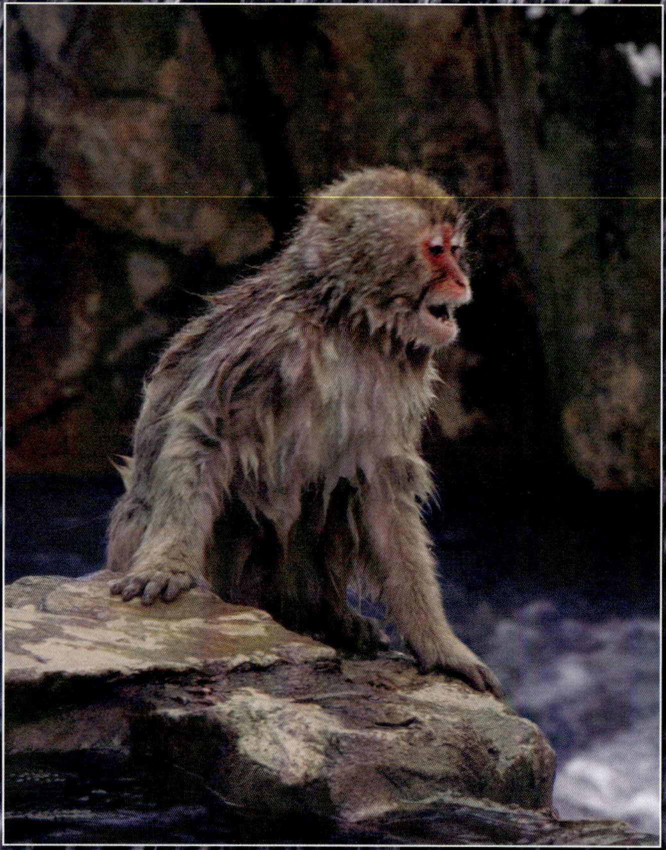

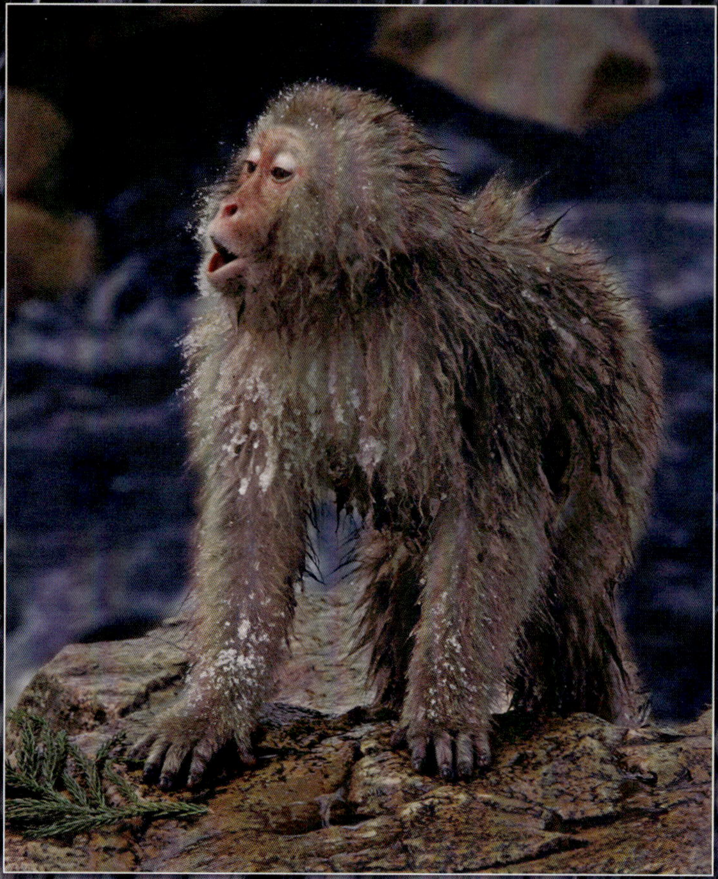

Some monkeys like to argue.

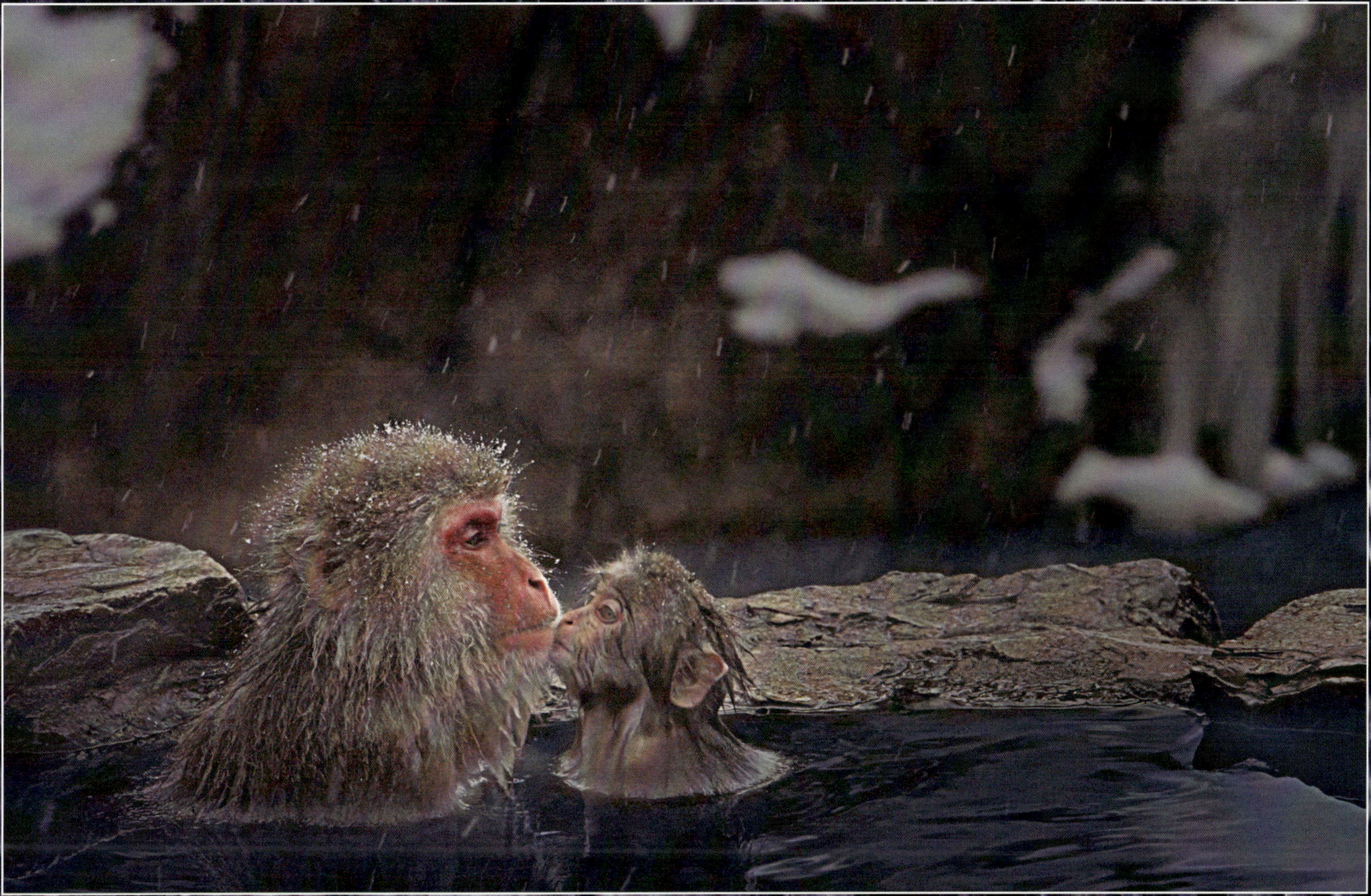

I prefer to kiss.

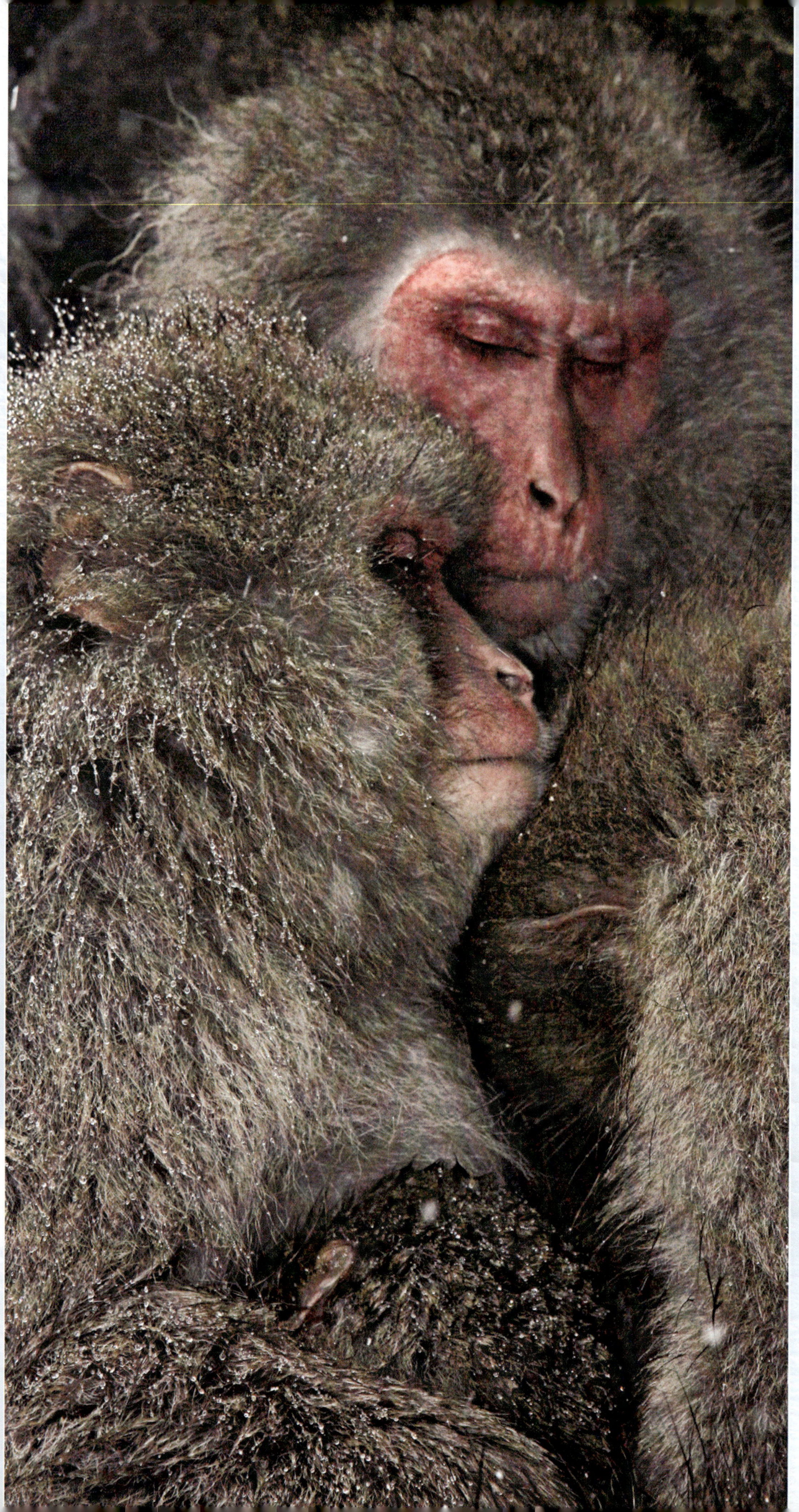

Snuggling for warmth

This is more exciting than a sleigh ride.

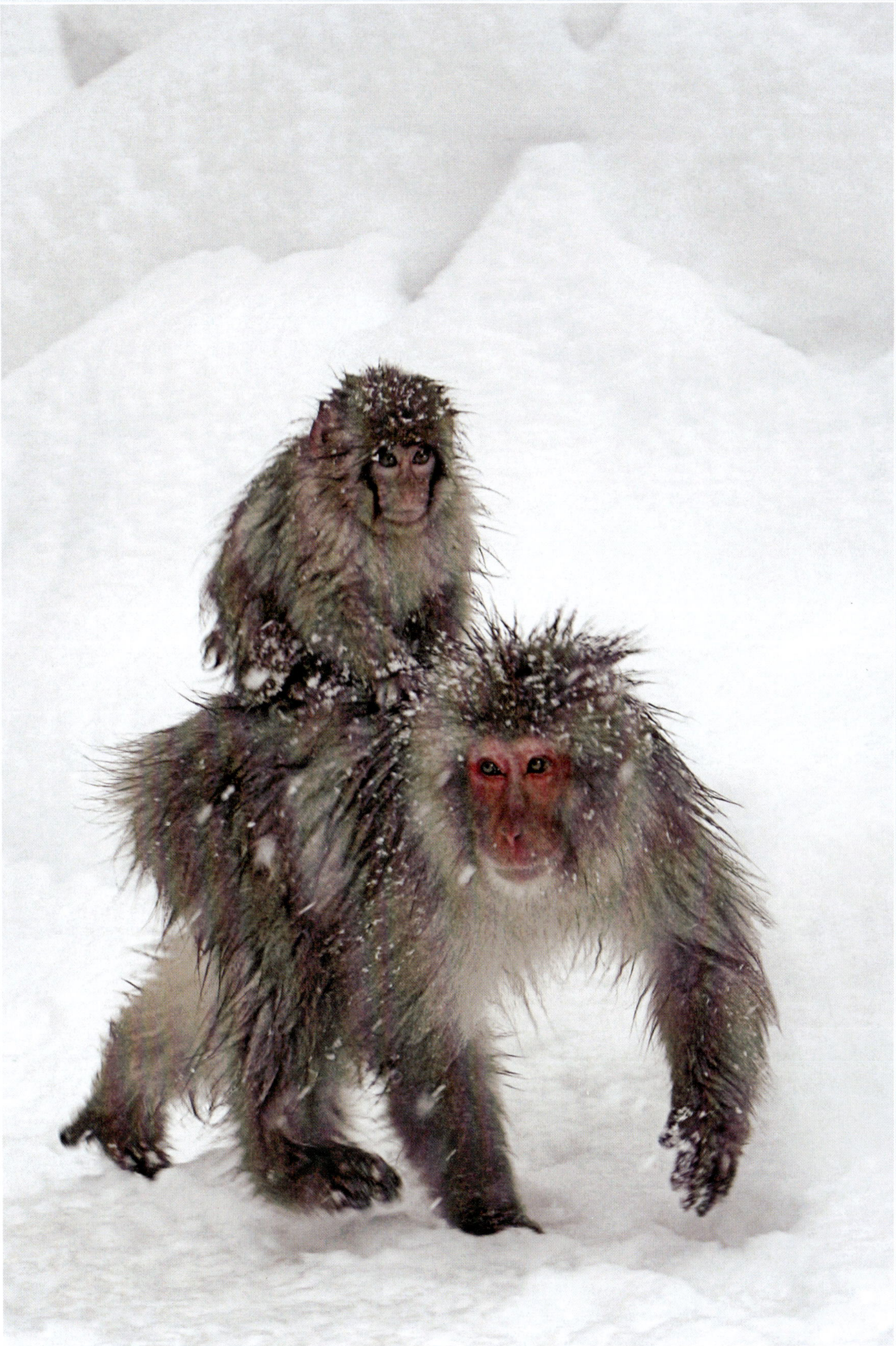

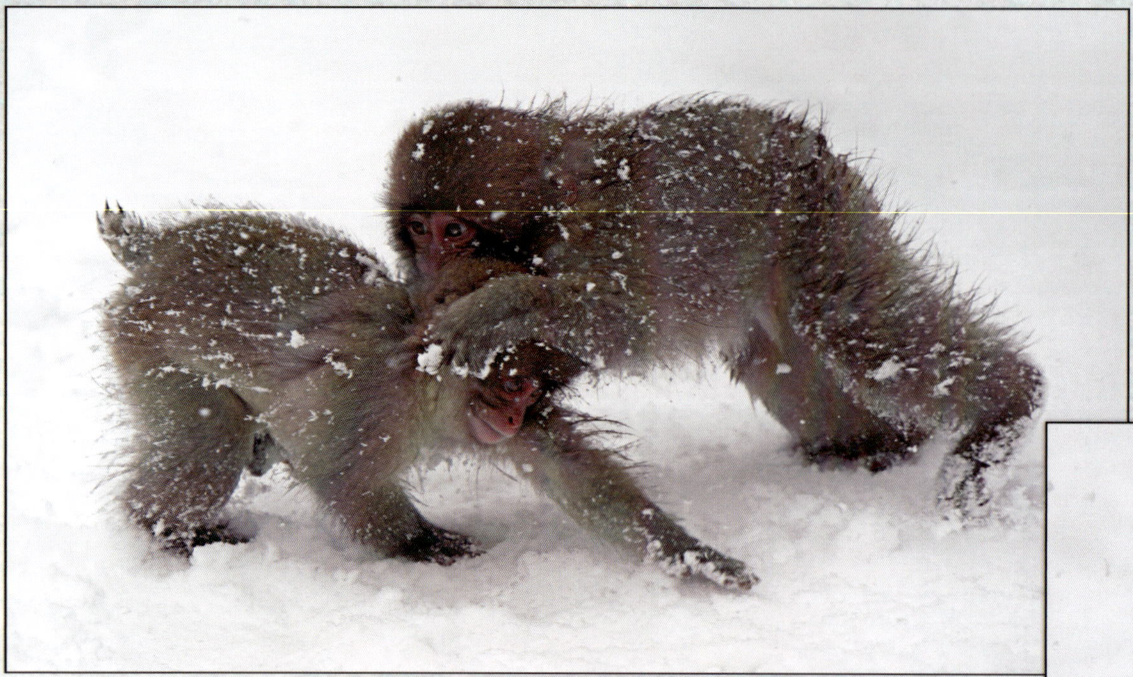

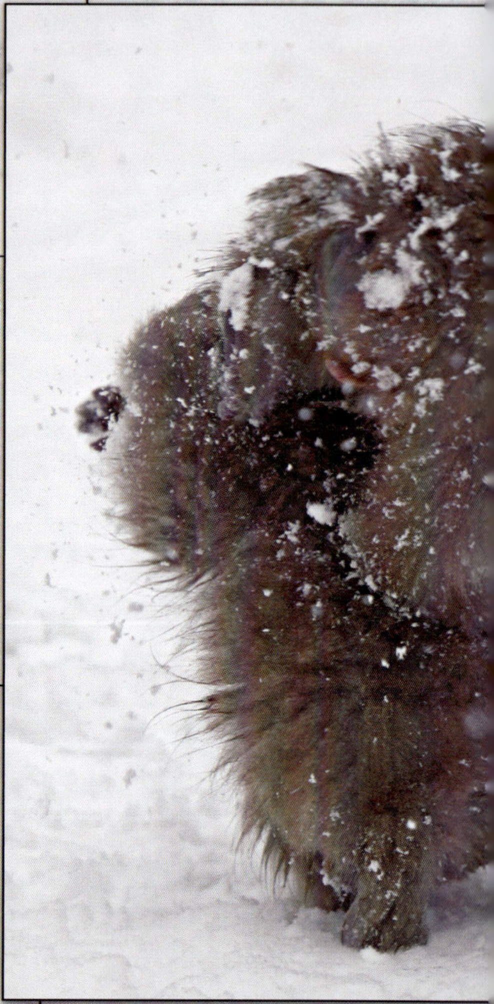

This is no monkey business.

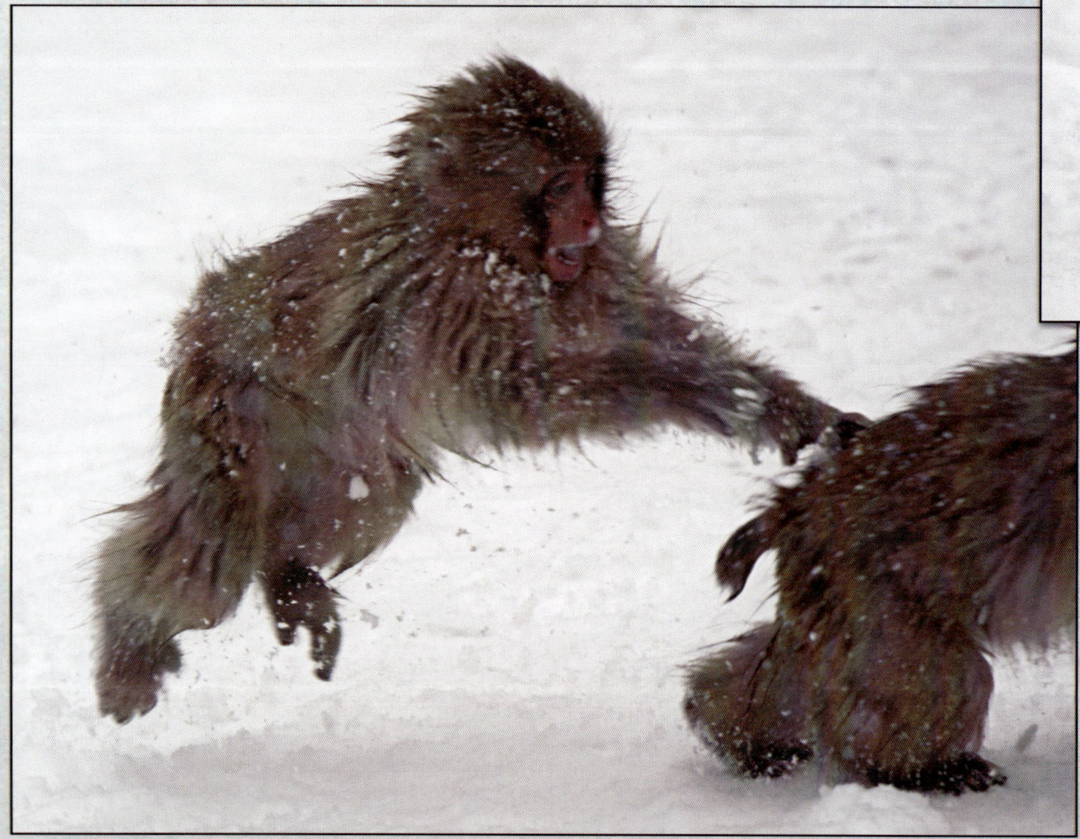

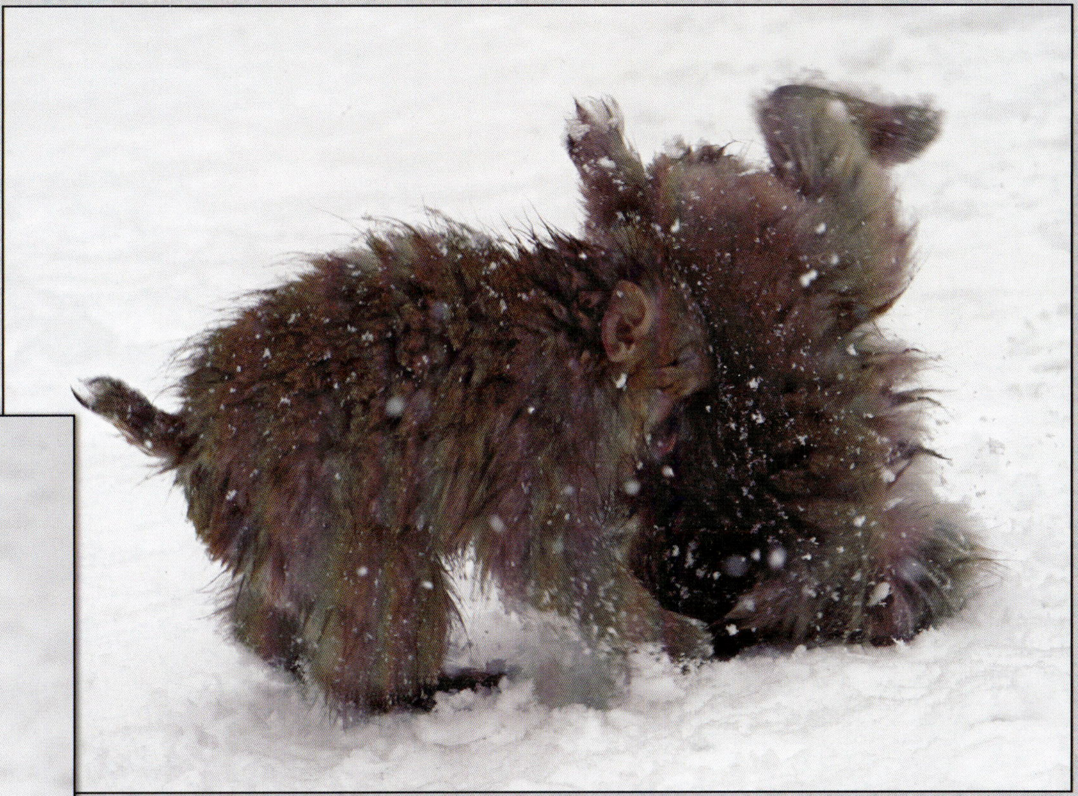

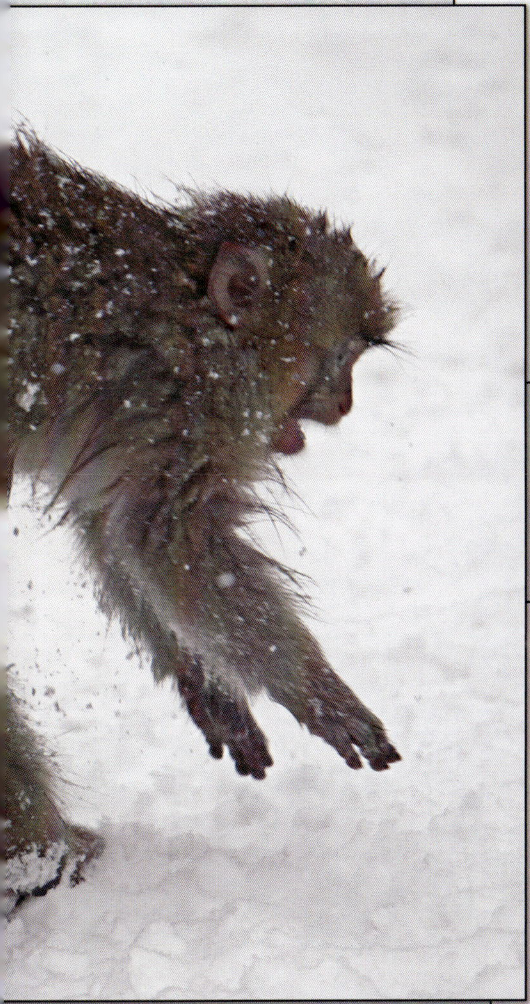

This is kung-fu fighting.

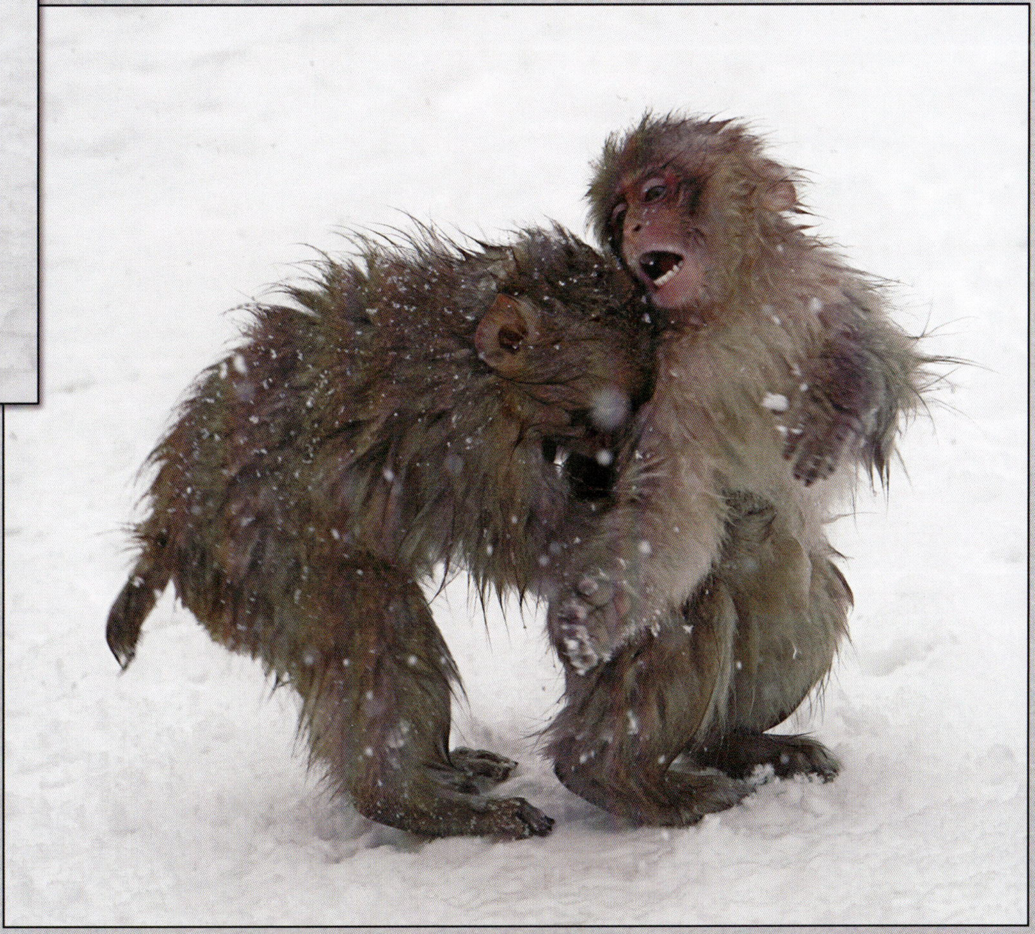

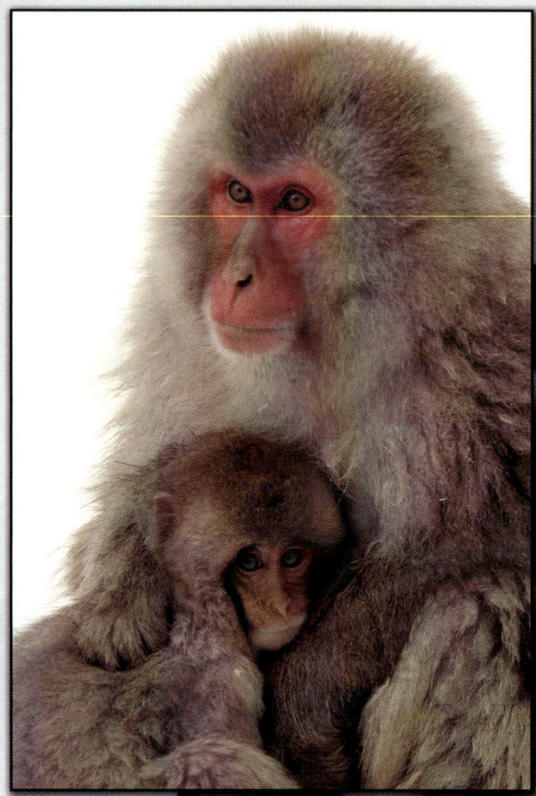

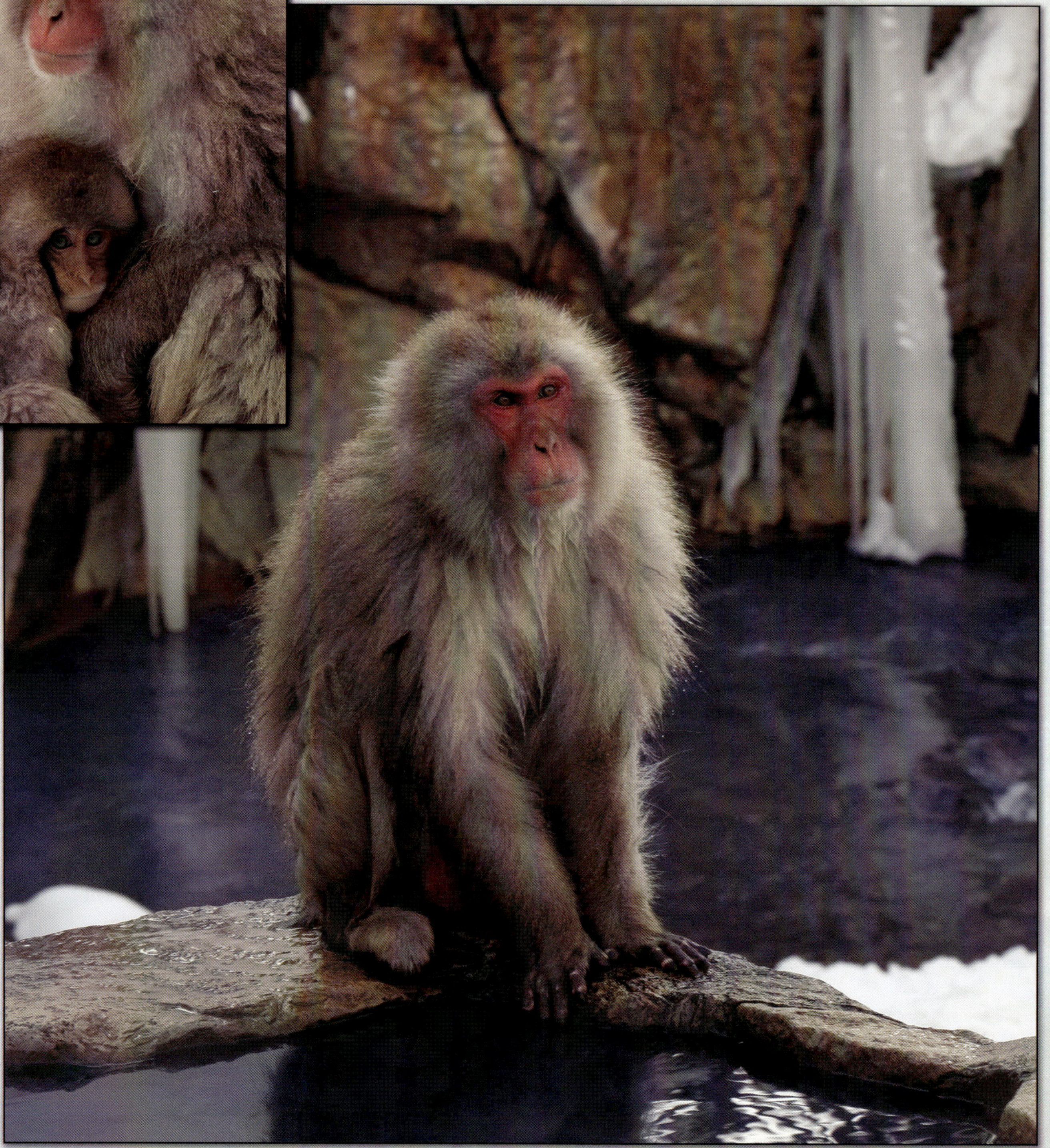

A winter break between snow storms is a blessing.

Relaxing in the hot spring is very soothing.

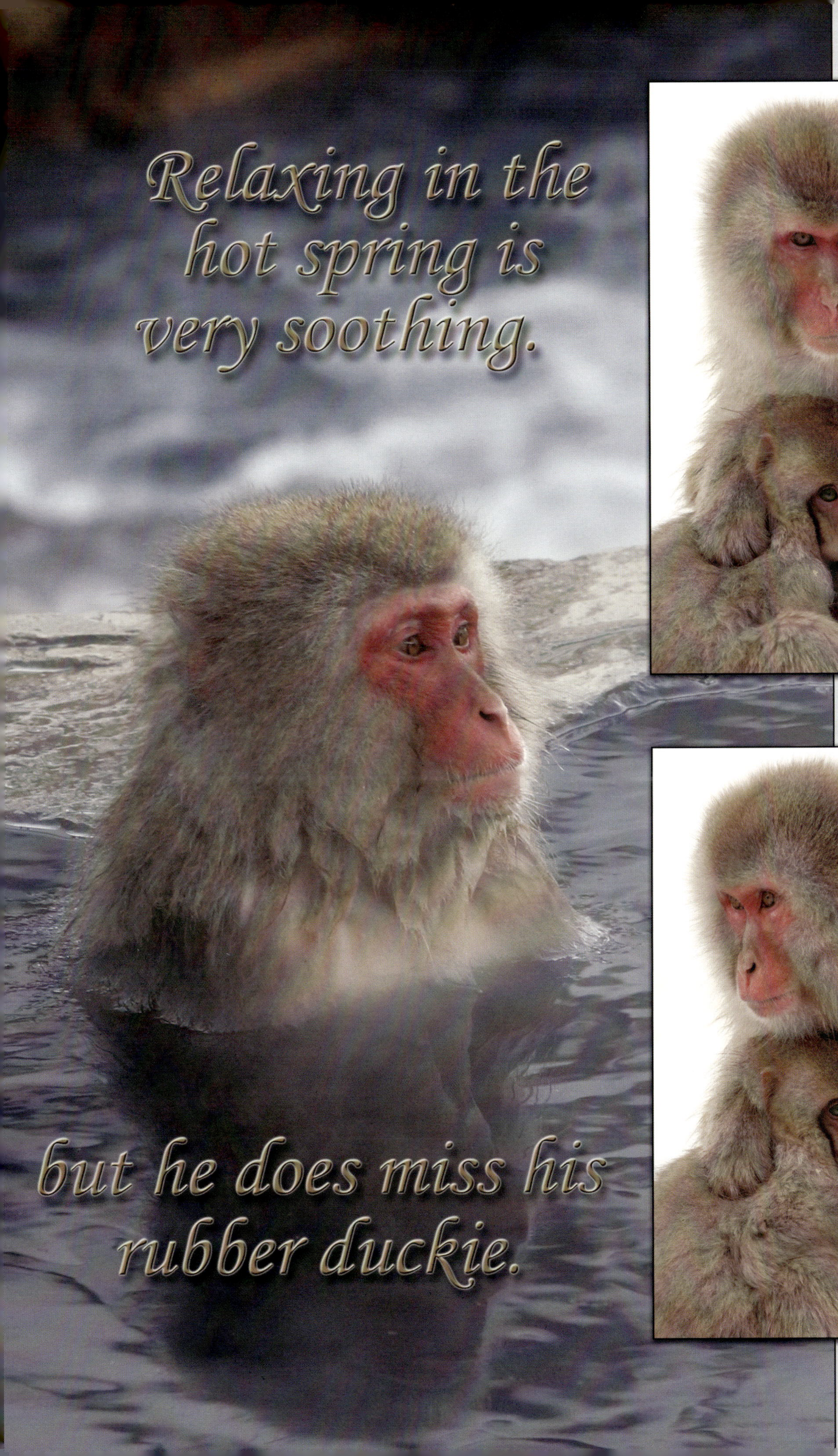

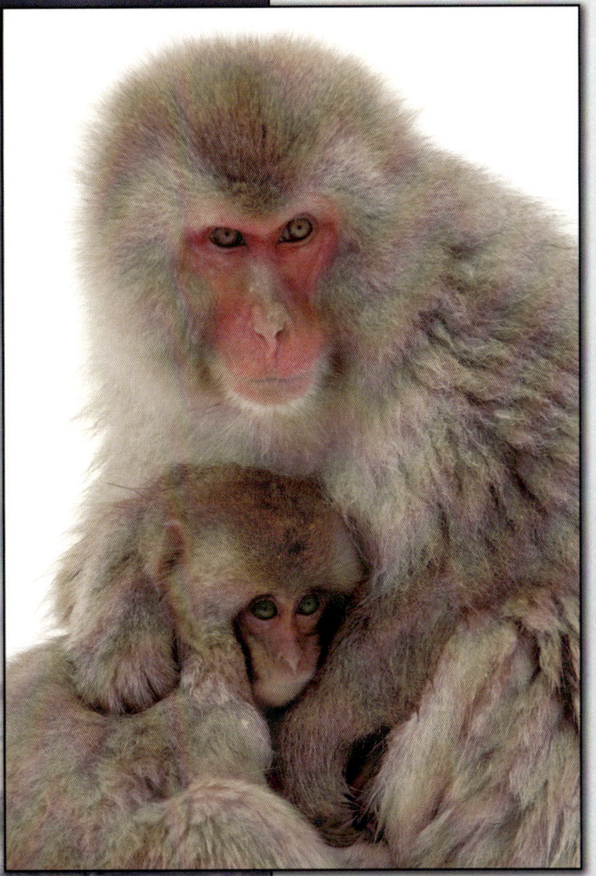

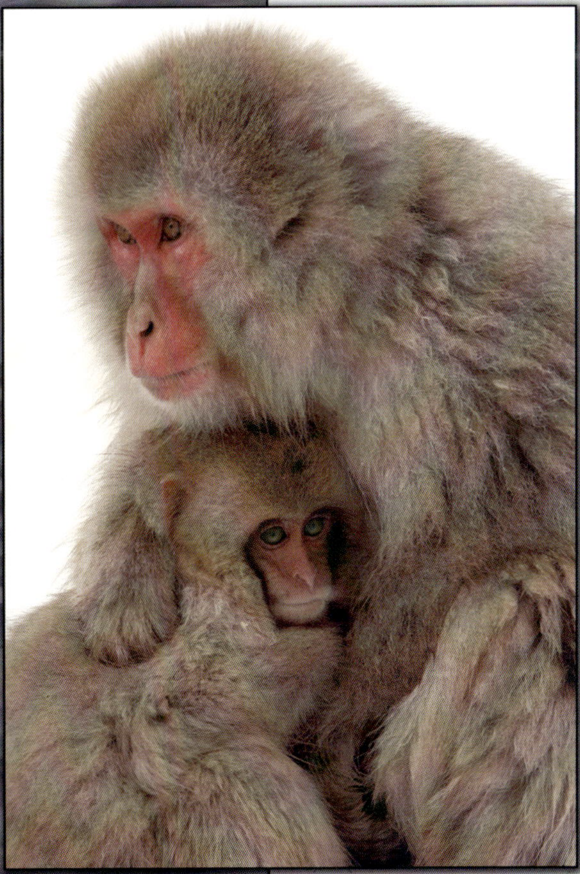

but he does miss his rubber duckie.

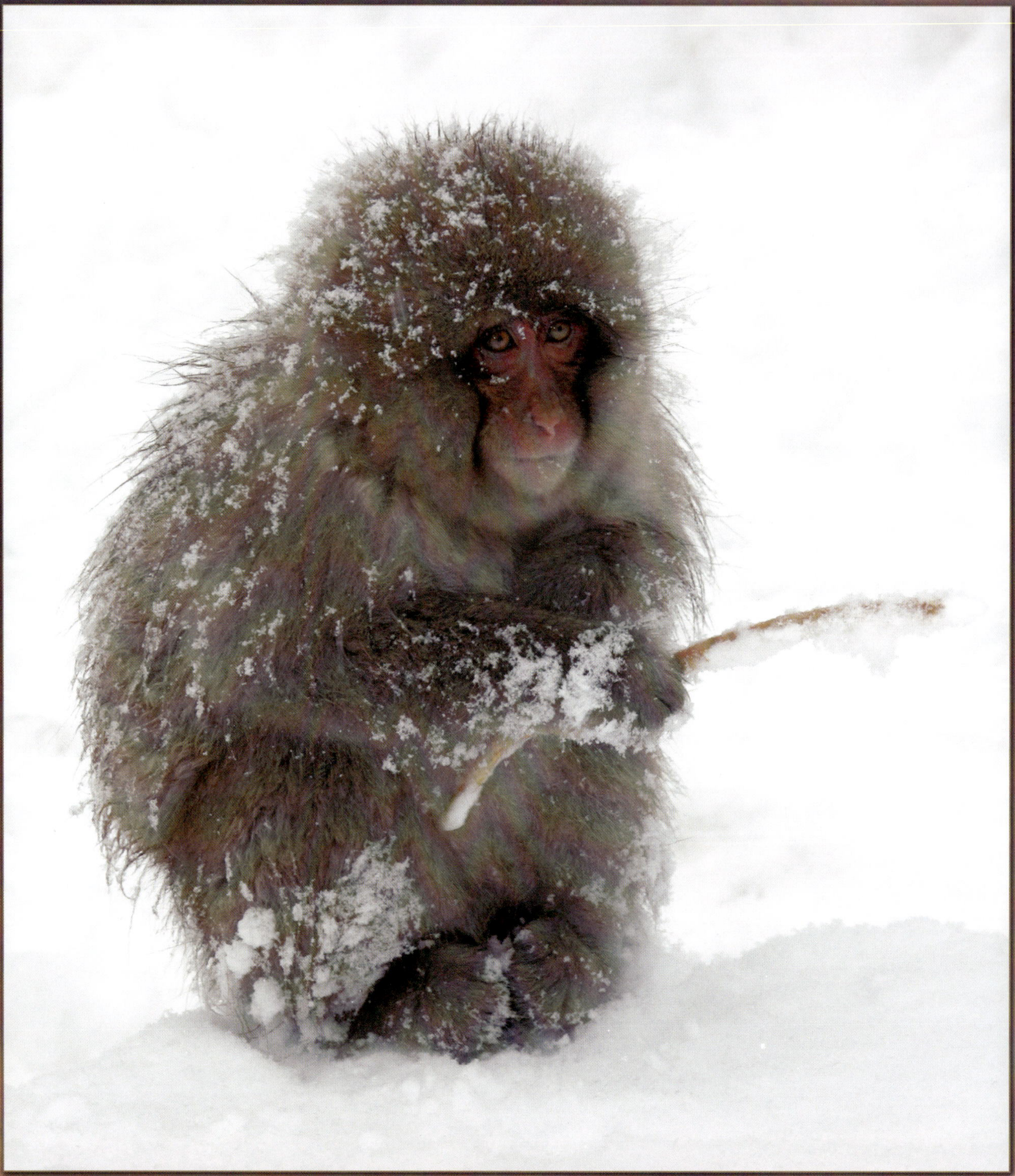

This monkey is snow fishing.

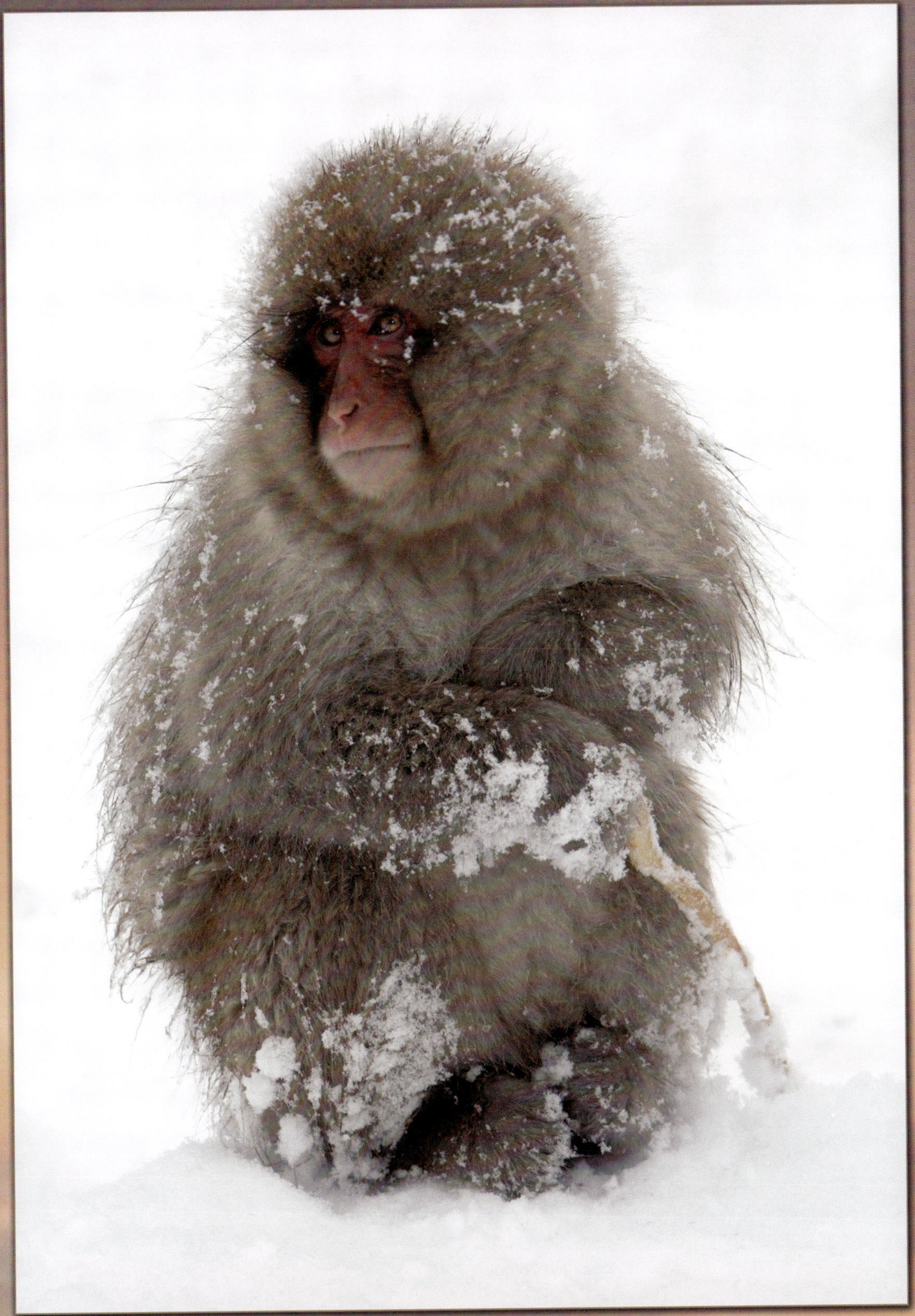

The monkey now has a cane.

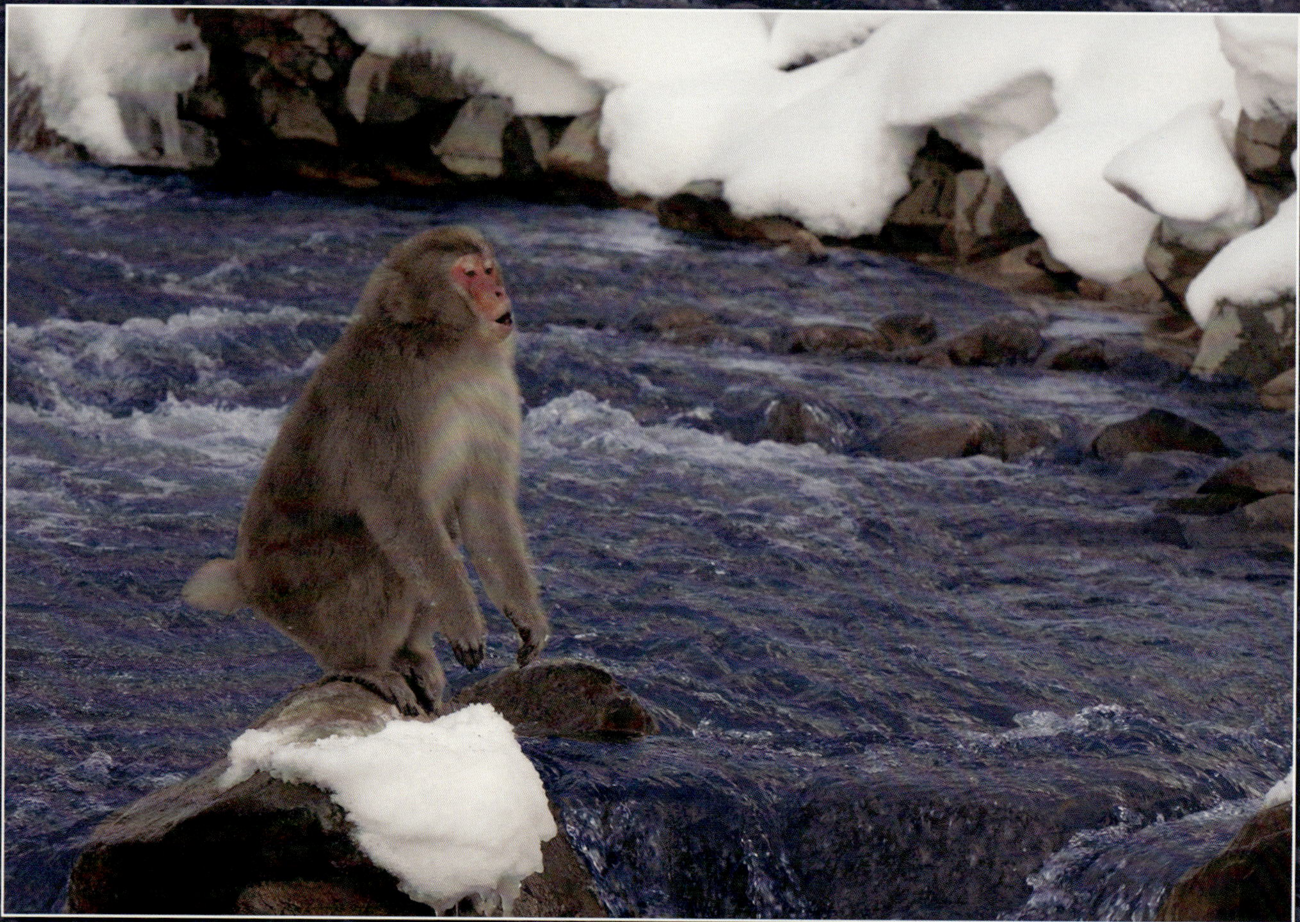

Snow monkeys don't like getting their toes wet.

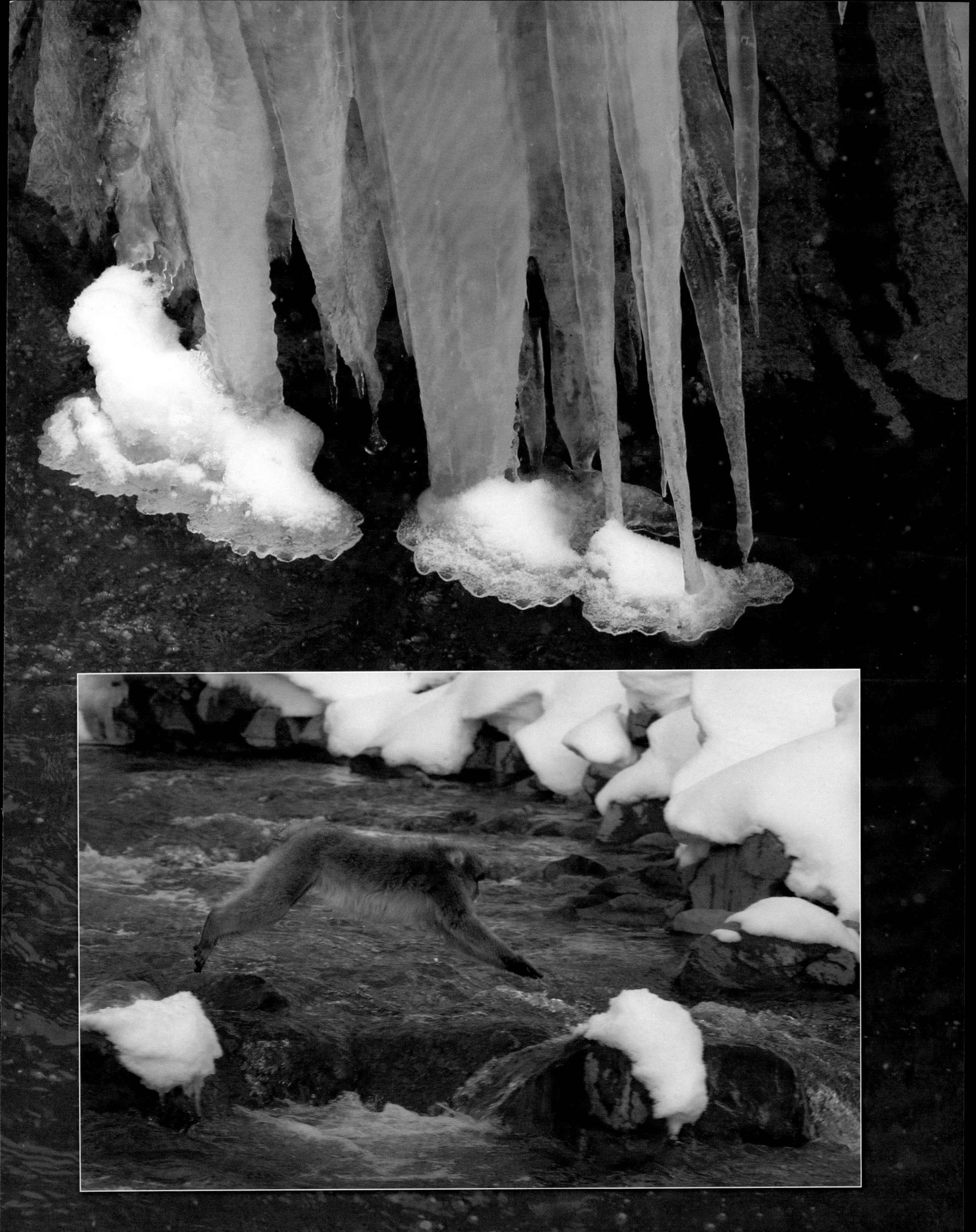

I have a very loving family.

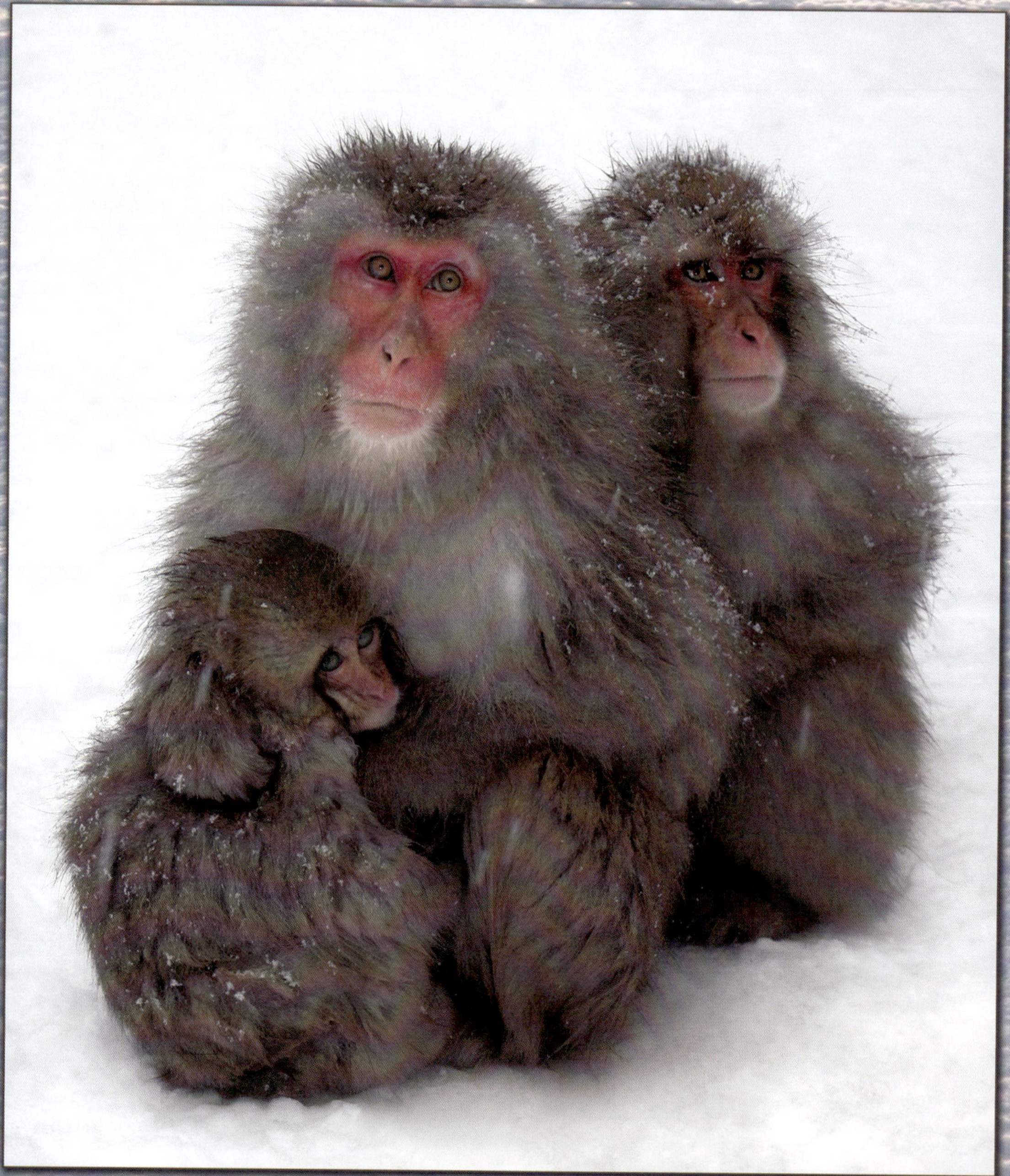

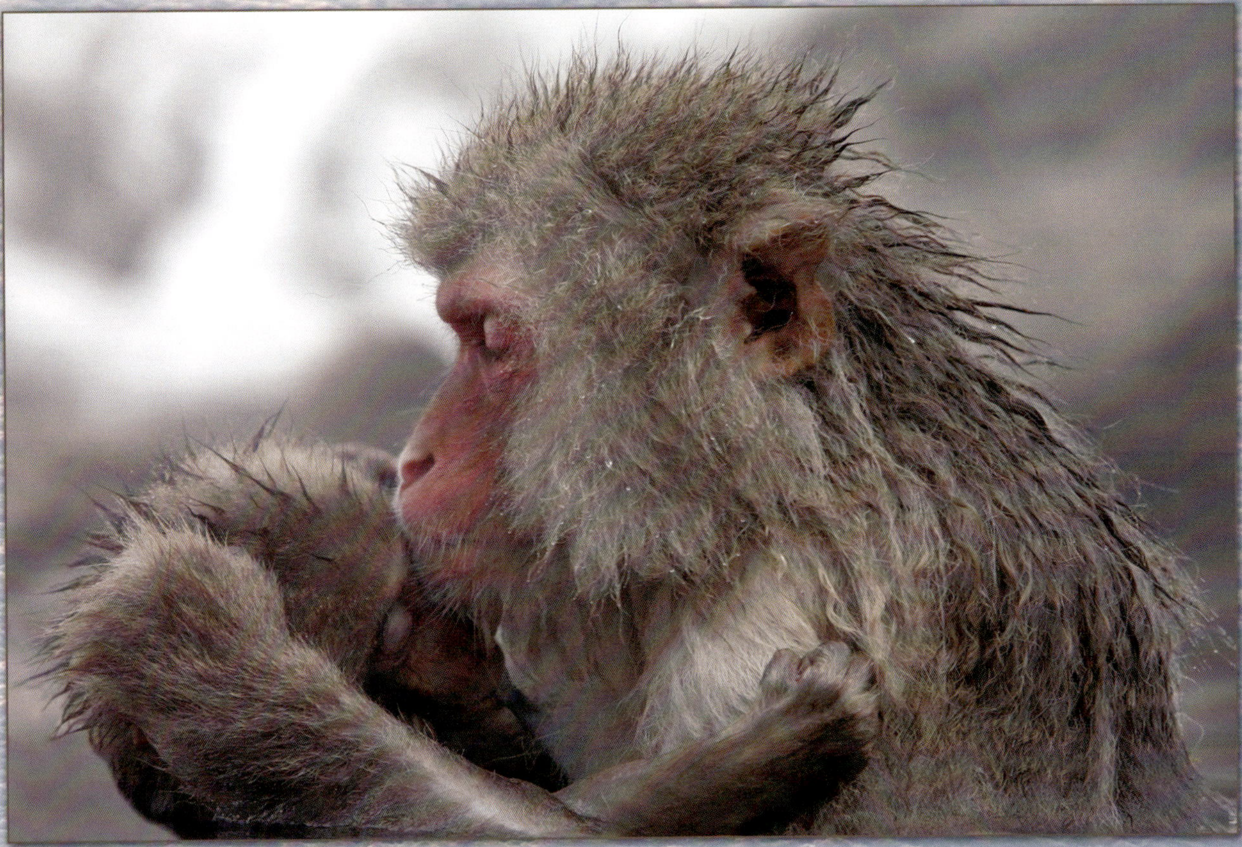
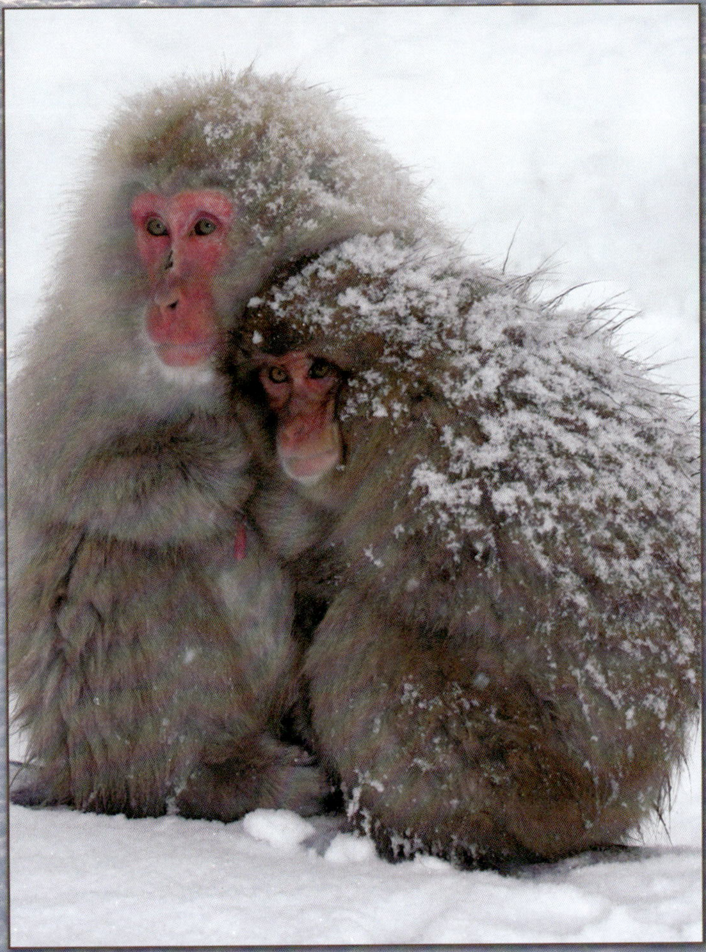

I am so thankful to my parents

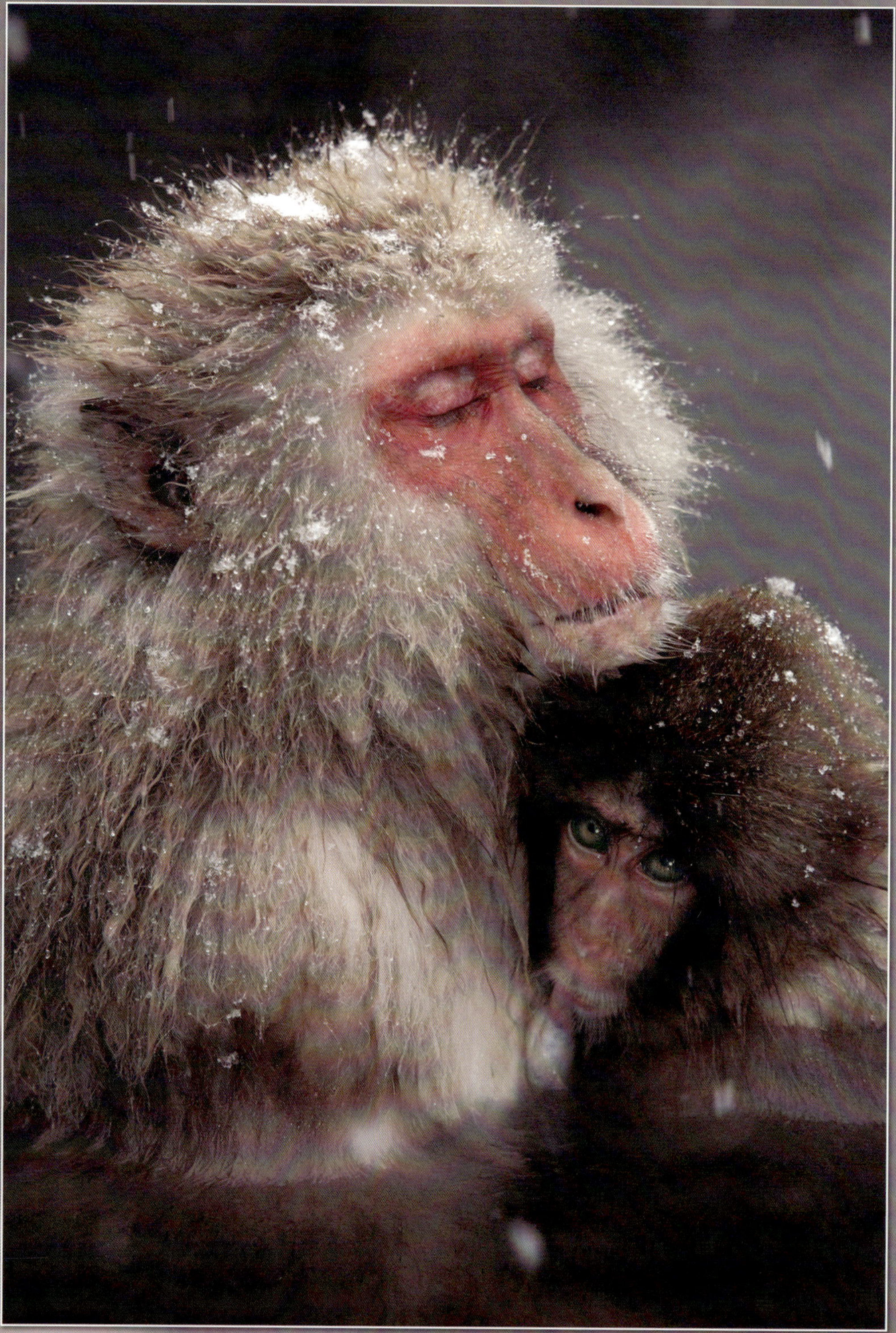

who love, feed, and protect me.

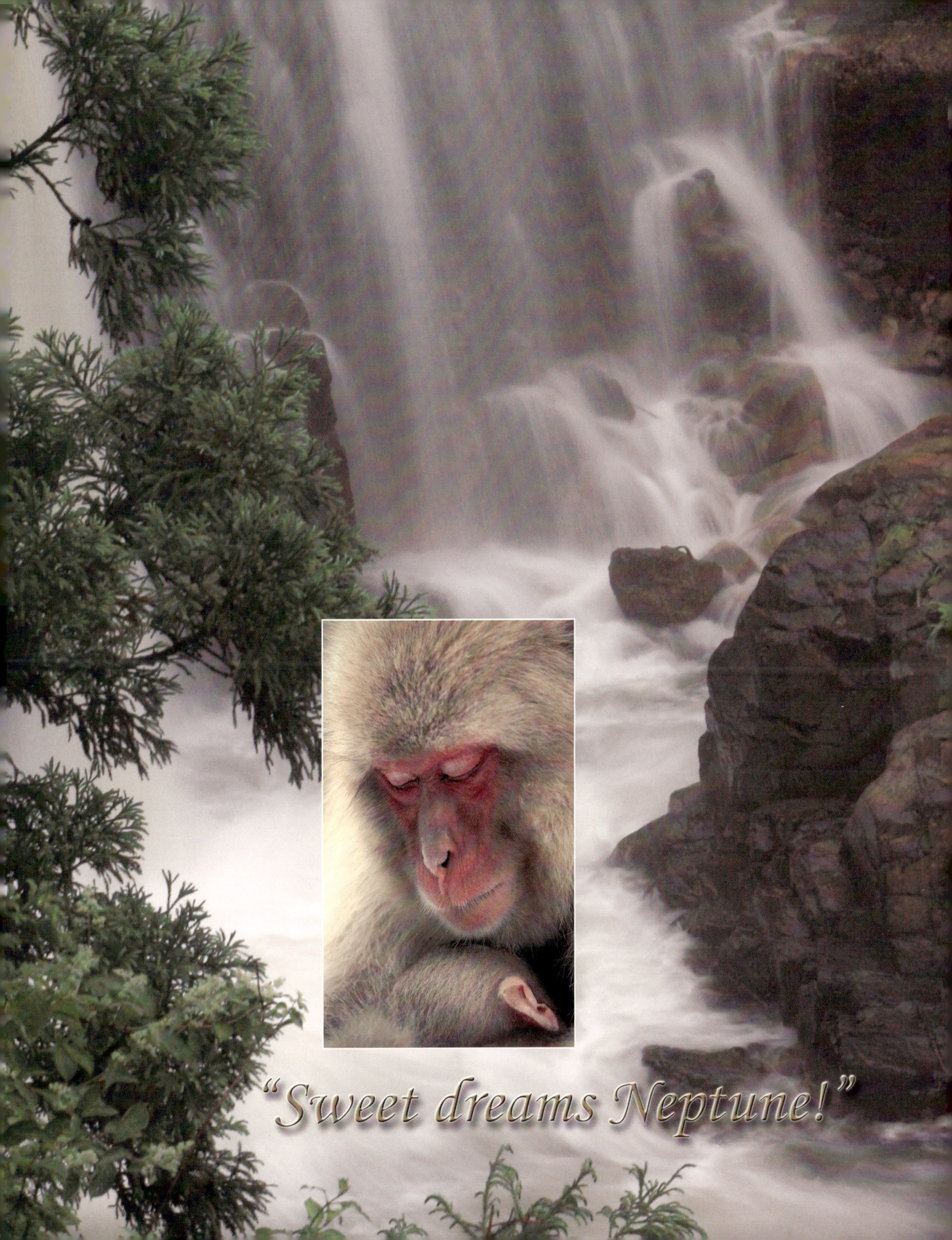

"Sweet dreams Neptune!"

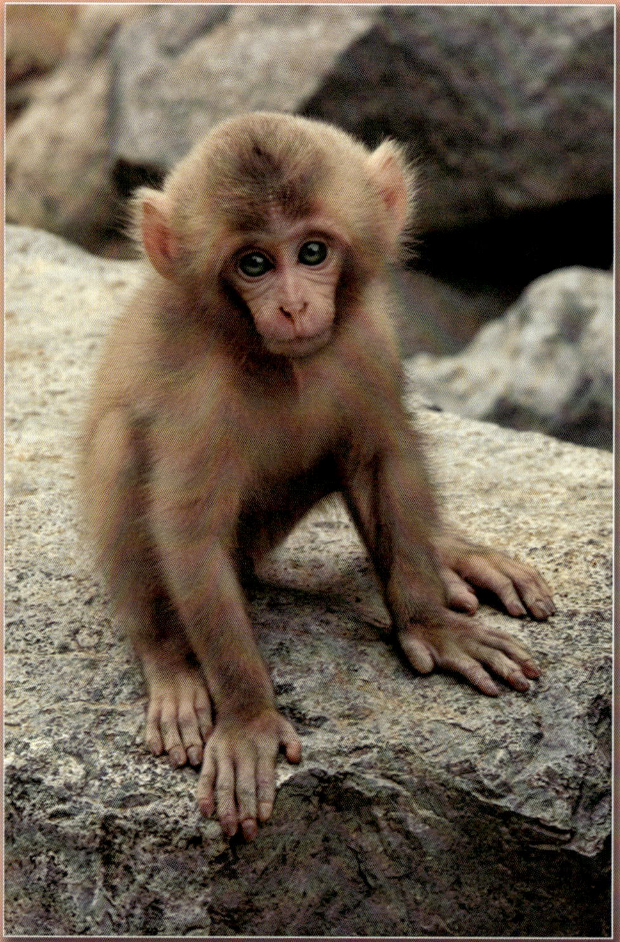

Published by:
Ostermeyer Photography
Allen, Texas
www.ostermeyer-photography.com